CW01369108

the PINK WHISK guide to BREAD MAKING

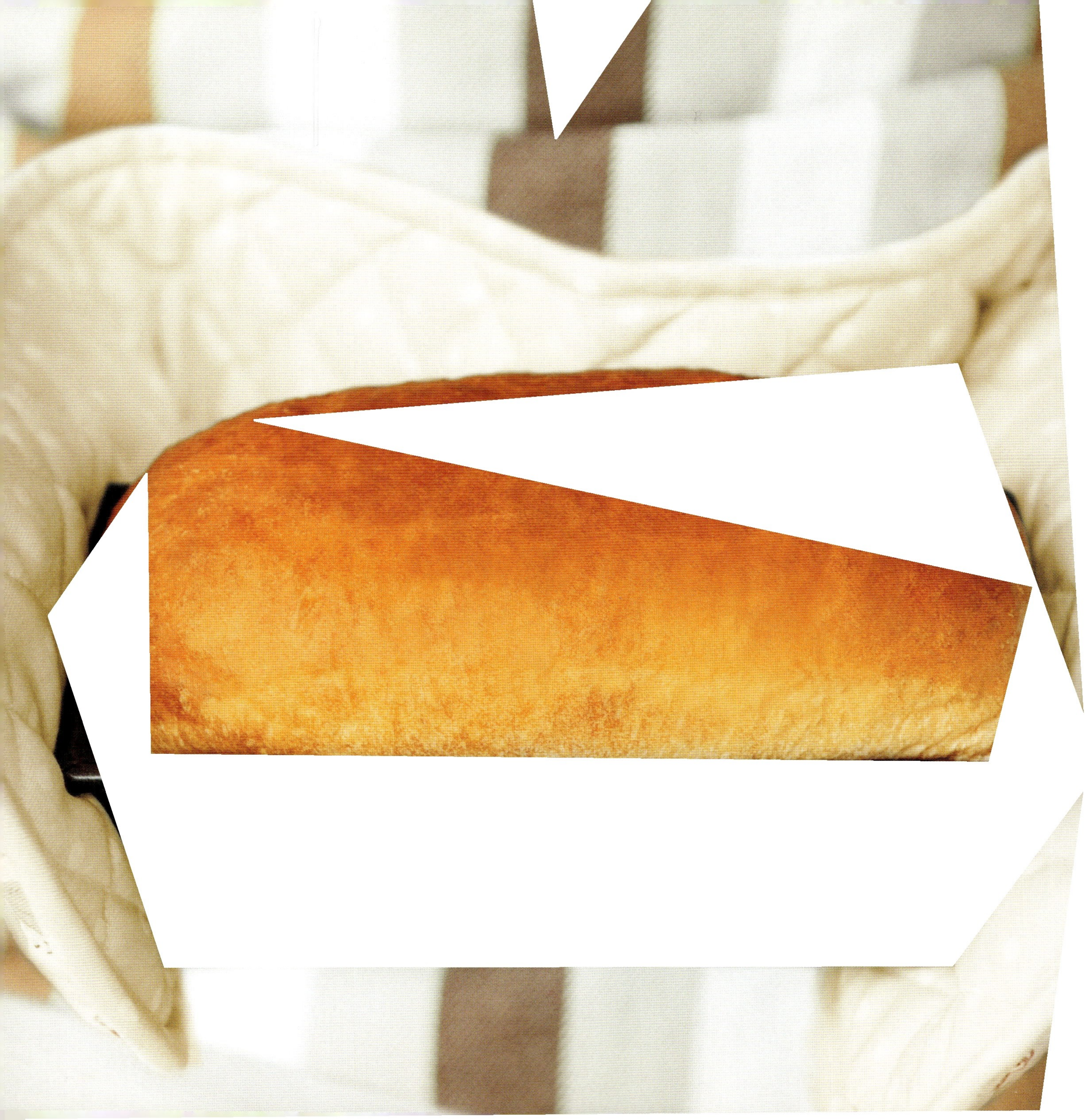

the PINK WHISK guide to BREAD MAKING

D&C
David and Charles

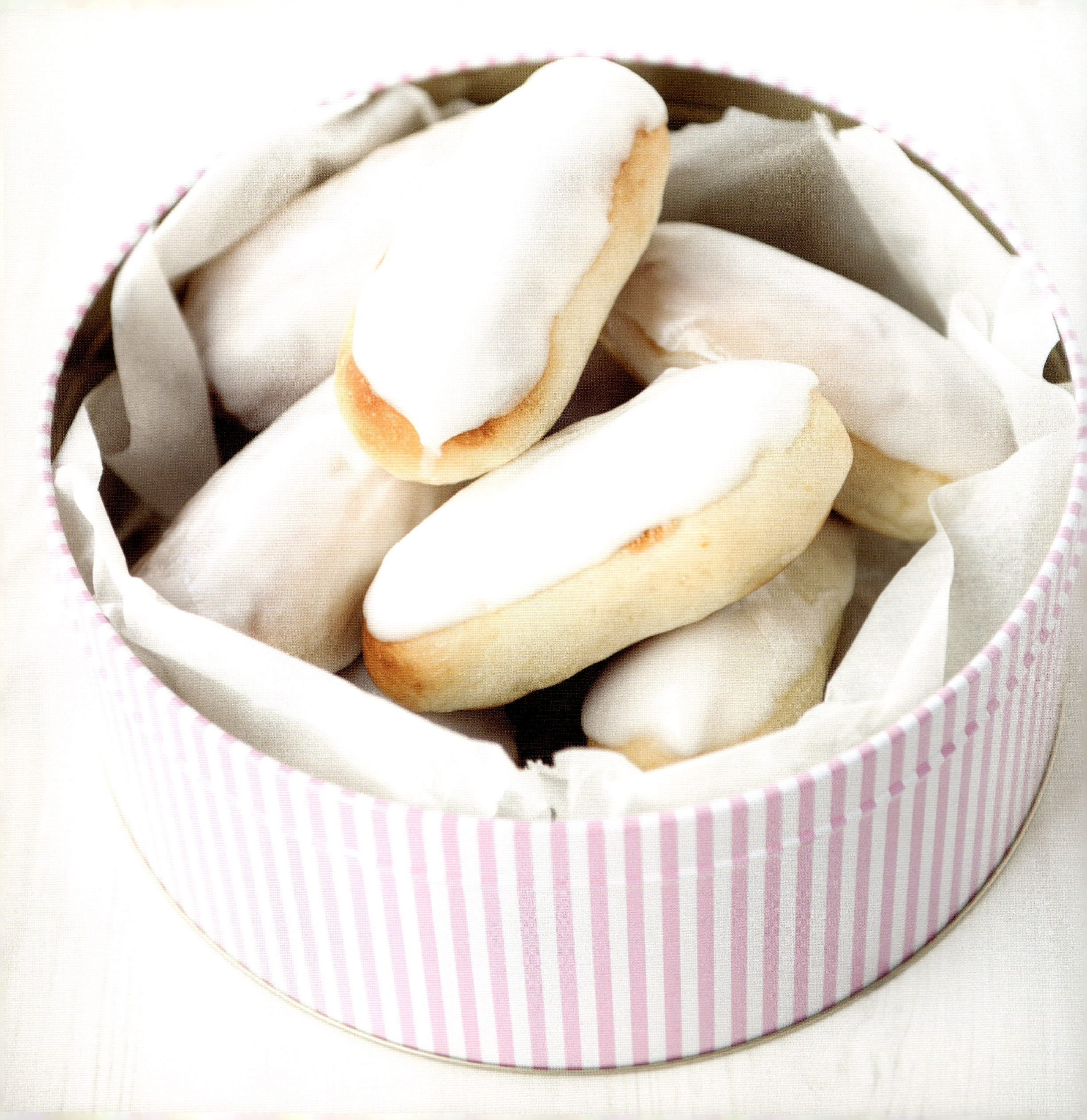

CONTENTS

Introduction	6
Equipment	8
Ingredients	10
Techniques	12
Troubleshooting	18
BRILLIANT BASICS	**20**
Basic White Loaf	22
Basic Brown Loaf	28
Quick White Rolls	30
Teacakes	34
BBQ Twist & Swirl Loaf	36
Cinnamon Twist & Swirl Loaf	40
Malthouse Loaf	42
Honey Oat Rolls	46
Bacon & Cheese Potato Bread	48
Chorizo & Chilli Potato Bread	52
Spiced Chocolate Orange Fingers	54
Iced Lemon Fingers	58
PERFECT PRE-FERMENT	**60**
Crusty Cobb	62
Tiger Bread	68
Seeded Multigrain Loaf	70
Maple & Pecan Loaf	74
Danish Apple Plait	76
Picnic Plait	80
Ciabatta with Olive Oil	82
Rosemary & Sea Salt Foccacia	86
Stilton & Cranberry Wheel	88
Chocolate & Hazelnut Wheel	92
FURTHER FAVOURITES	**94**
Savoury Bagels	96
Sweet Cinnamon & Cranberry Bagels	102
Challah	104
Herby Braided Loaf	110
Brioche	112
Brioche Pizza	116
Danish Pastry – Raisin Whirls	118
Croissants	122
Suppliers & Acknowledgements	124
Index	126

INTRODUCTION

Hello! Welcome to *The Pink Whisk Guide to Bread Making*. There is one thing I am sure of: you can't beat the satisfaction of baking (and eating) your own loaf, or the delicious aroma it creates as it bakes in your oven.

Bread making isn't a labour-intensive process but you do need a bit of time and some forward planning. Follow the step-by-step instructions in the recipes and you'll soon be on your way to a fantastic loaf. It doesn't have to be perfect – it's homemade after all – and that's why you'll be so proud of it.

Like any type of baking, bread making can be full of pitfalls, but as I fell into most of them while devising the recipes here, you can avoid them. It's worthwhile investing time in understanding what makes a good loaf and for me that generally means learning by my mistakes! I'd highly recommend reading through the techniques and troubleshooting sections for lots of tips before you get going.

This book is full of bread recipes for loaves of all shapes, to suit all tastes, but it isn't just about the recipes: it's about making all of your bread making even better than before. I've tried to jam in as many tips and tricks as possible, plus explanations of why you should do a certain something at a specific stage – the sort of thing that's missed out of most recipe methods. You'll then be able to apply these techniques to all of your bread making – and you'll be turning out delicious homemade loaves in next to no time.

The recipes are in three sections by method; straightforward doughs in Brilliant Basics, doughs made using a pre-ferment in Perfect Pre-Ferments, and recipes that have slightly different methods in Further Favourites. There are breads for every occasion, each with its own variation to show you how things can be mixed up a little bit to create something different. I hope these will give you inspiration to dream up your own loaves and recipes. Jump right in and experiment with your own favourite ingredients and bread additions, and don't be afraid of using a recipe as the basis for something else. Bake it smaller in rolls or bigger as a loaf, go free-form or shape it in a tin: you'll learn all sorts as you go and I'll be here to help you along the way.

Ruth x

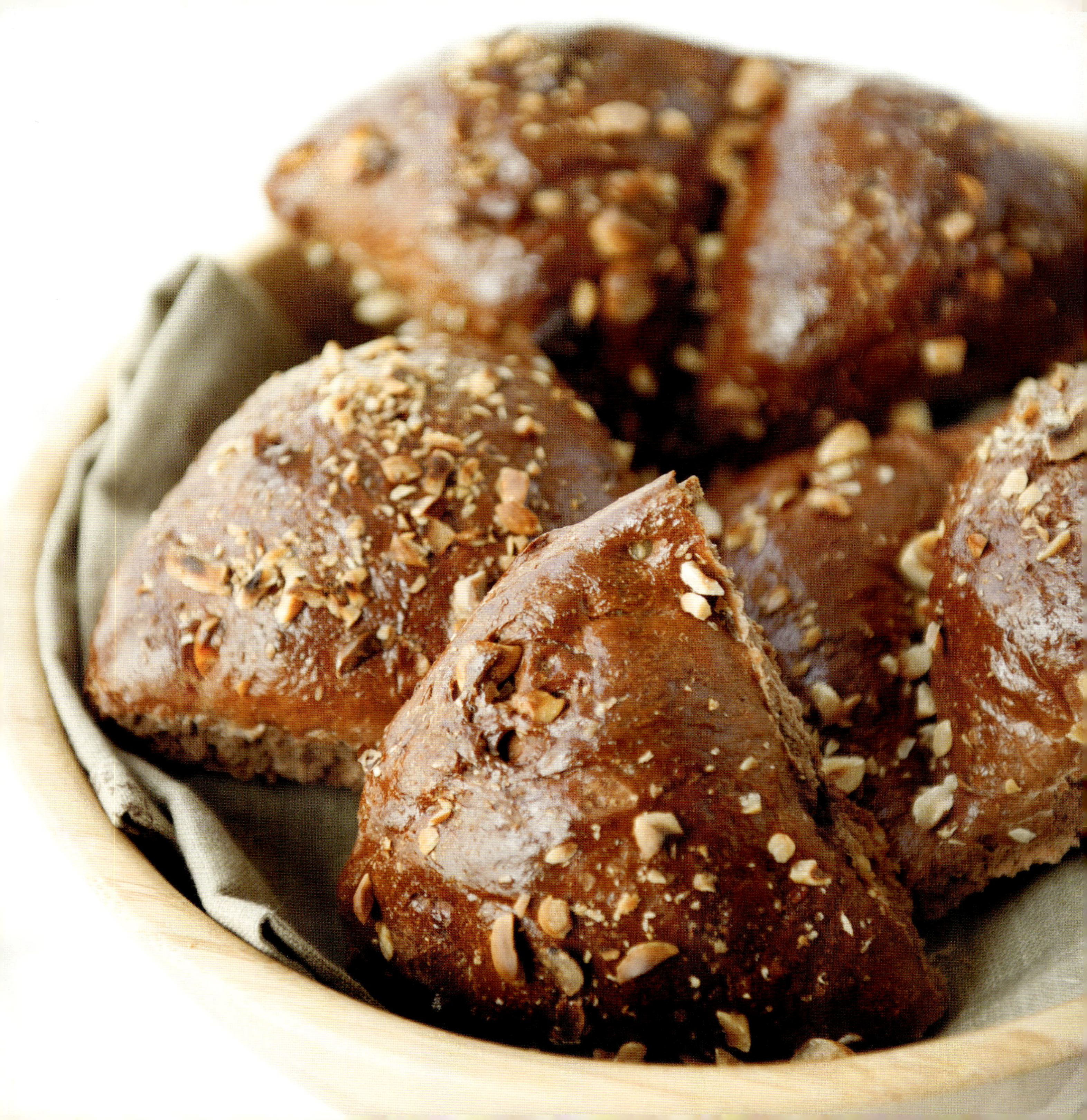

EQUIPMENT

Having the right equipment to hand makes baking the best thing since sliced bread! Special items needed in the recipes such as a loaf tin (pan) or stand mixer are listed alongside ingredients. Kitchen essentials needed for every recipe such as scales, bowls, dish towels and cling film (plastic wrap) are not listed as most kitchens will have these items available.

TIP
Bread should be sliced with a sharp serrated bread knife in a sawing motion – this stops the bread becoming compacted when it is cut.

- Flour shaker
- Pastry brush
- Cling film (plastic wrap)
- Baking (parchment) paper
- Digital kitchen scales
- Measuring spoons
- Blades
- Oven thermometer
- Plastic dough scraper
- Serrated bread knife
- Metal dough blade
- Sharp knife

Stand mixer

Measuring jug

Reusable silicone sheet (bake-o-glide)

900g (2lb) loaf tin (pan)

Baking sheet

Dish towel

Mixing bowl

TIP
Good quality tins (pans) will always stand you in good stead: they distribute heat evenly and will give you a better bake. Look after them and they'll look after you! They should be hand washed in warm soapy water – don't go sticking them in the dishwasher. They will build up a patina over time that makes their performance better.

INGREDIENTS

STRONG / BREAD FLOURS
The main ingredient in bread making, bread flour is higher in protein than plain (all-purpose) flour and therefore produces the high gluten level needed for bread making. Flours for bread making will vary in protein content but are generally over 11 per cent and often up to 15 per cent.

Strong white bread flour
It's worth sticking with one type of strong white bread flour as different brands will vary in their absorbency of liquid. That way you'll get to know your flour and can note down any recipe adjustments you need to make for next time.

Malted Bread Flour
A mix of strong wholemeal (whole wheat) bread flour, malted wheat flakes and grains for sweeter, nuttier loaves.

Wholemeal (whole wheat) bread flour
This has slightly lower gluten than white bread flour, which is why it is often mixed with white bread flour in recipes, rather than used on its own. It will absorb much more liquid than white bread flour. It has a nutty taste, and as it contains wheat germ and bran it's good for you. The bran content will inhibit the rise in the dough so it will need longer to prove and bake, and will produce a denser, coarser loaf.

YEAST
Yeast is used to make the dough rise by aerating it, which gives it a light, open texture. The yeast needs warmth,

moisture and nutrients (starch from the flour plus sugar and salt) to multiply and grow. Too much of any of these and it will be killed, resulting in a failed loaf.

All of the recipes in this book can be made using any type of yeast. Both fresh and dried yeast will need to be soaked in a little of the liquid from the recipe until the mixture starts to bubble and froth. Calculate the amounts needed using the following conversion:

1 tsp fast action yeast = 6.5g (¼ oz) fresh yeast = 3.5g (1½ tsp) dried yeast

Fast action yeast
Also referred to as quick, instant, fast dried and easy blend yeast, this is often sold in sachets to help keep its freshness. It is my preferred choice for yeast and the recipes here all use it. It doesn't need reconstituting with water first and can be added directly to the bowl with the other ingredients. Be sure to check your yeast is within its use-by date.

Dried yeast
This yeast is in a pellet form, which needs to be soaked in water before using.

Fresh yeast
This can be difficult to get hold of, but try health food or wholefood shops – they will often have it in the chiller cabinet. It comes in a block and is beige in colour with a creamy texture and yeasty smell. It keeps for approximately 1 week in the fridge but will quickly discolour, dry out and lose efficacy so buy it as you need it.

SALT
This enhances the flavour of bread, helps to strengthen the gluten, and acts as a preservative. Too much will kill the yeast. It won't harm fast action yeast if it comes into contact with it in the mixing bowl but be careful with fresh and reconstituted dried yeast, placing them away from salt in the bowl prior to mixing. Sea salt can be used instead of table salt but it should be finely ground first.

SUGAR
Caster (superfine) or granulated sugar in savoury doughs acts as source of food for the yeast. It can be used in a greater quantity to sweeten doughs and darken a crust. It is sometimes added in the form of honey, treacle (molasses) or malt extract which will not only add sweetness but also flavour and colour.

LIQUIDS
Some doughs are more hydrated than others and liquid can be added in all sorts of forms; water, milk, apple juice and so on. Liquids should be warmed to blood temperature so that the temperature of your finished dough is warm enough for the yeast to be activated. Too hot and the yeast will be killed, too cold and the dough will be slow to rise. One part boiling water to two parts cold water gives the correct temperature. For a pre-ferment cold liquid is fine. Milk will provide a finer textured crumb than water due to the fat content. The liquid measurements in the recipes should be used as a guide – as you get to know your flour you may need to make little adjustments. Just make sure you note them down for next time.

Weighing liquids
Weighing is the most accurate method for measuring your liquid content. Some kitchen scales will have settings for measuring water and milk in millilitres or fluid ounces. Cold water weighs the same as it measures in volume, for example 100ml = 100g; 4fl oz = 4oz. Other liquids such as milk have different volume to weight ratios.

FATS
Fat in a dough will produce a loaf with a finer texture and will help with the keeping quality when baked. It can be added as butter, eggs, vegetable, sunflower or olive oil. Recipes in this book use salted butter. Eggs are free-range and always large, and when used in high proportions, such as in Brioche, the dough will need longer to rise.

TECHNIQUES

MAKING A ROUGH DOUGH
Dry ingredients are placed in a large mixing bowl, and any ingredients added with a measuring spoon should be level spoonfuls. Wet ingredients are measured out as per the recipe (which is best done by weight for accuracy), warmed as necessary and then added to the dry ingredients in the bowl. Mixing by hand is the easiest (but stickiest!) way to combine the ingredients to form a rough dough. Spread out and then bend your fingers to make your hand into a claw shape and start to work together the wet and dry ingredients until they form a shaggy dough which is then ready to be kneaded. A rough dough can also be mixed with a wooden spoon or strong silicone spatula if preferred.

MIXING A PRE-FERMENT
Liquid for a pre-ferment doesn't need to be warm as the yeast is allowed to develop over a longer period of time. Stir together the ingredients for a pre-ferment in a bowl large enough to allow for some expansion in size. The mixture will still be a little lumpy but make sure there are no pockets of flour. Cover and set aside in a cool position to develop for a minimum of 4 hours, or overnight in the fridge. After developing, the pre-ferment is mixed with more flour and other ingredients to form the final dough. Most recipes can be changed to benefit from a pre-ferment: simply mix together half of the flour needed in the recipe with the full amount of yeast and liquid to make the pre-ferment. Once developed, mix the pre-ferment with the other half of the flour and any other ingredients listed to form your dough.

KNEADING
This is the process of working the dough to distribute the yeast evenly and develop the essential gluten. Kneading stretches out the gluten into long strands until the dough is smooth and much more elastic. The more it is worked, the stretchier it becomes.

Kneading by hand
Allow yourself enough space on the work surface; clear any clutter out of the way so you have room to work. Avoid putting any flour on the work surface as this extra flour will be incorporated into the dough and cause it to tighten, making your finished loaf dense. Don't be afraid of a sticky dough: some of the very best loaves are made with a sticky dough and as you knead you will soon find it gets easier and less sticky.

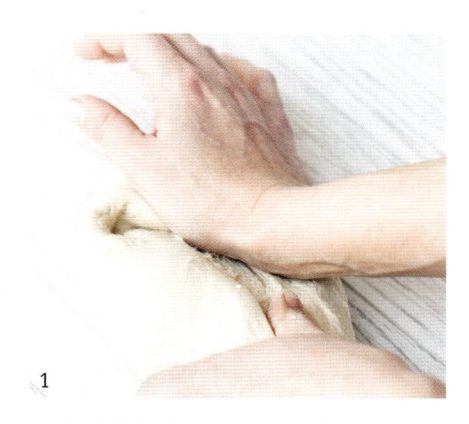

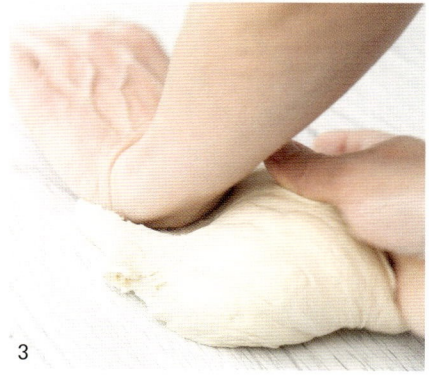

Place the ball of rough dough onto your work surface. Using the heel of your right hand push the dough out and forward diagonally to the right **(1)**, flip the stretched part back onto the ball of dough **(2)**, and repeat the action with the heel of your left hand, stretching it diagonally out to the left **(3)**. To begin with the dough won't move very far without breaking as you stretch. The more you knead the further it will begin to stretch. As the dough becomes smoother and more elastic turn the ball of dough slightly after every right and left push.

Kneaded dough will become smooth, satiny and more elastic in an average of 10 minutes. If your technique is a little lacklustre you will need to knead for longer. When you think it is ready you can test it by forming a ball and prodding with a fingertip: if it springs back into position it's ready for the first prove.

For extremely soft and sticky doughs which will barely form a ball, kneading can be done by grasping and lifting with fingertips, flicking back down onto the main portion of dough and continuing until it becomes smooth. Lift the dough higher and higher as the elasticity grows. If the thought of this puts you off bread making consider mixing it in the machine.

Kneading by machine

By all means use a stand mixer, or a bread machine on the dough setting to mix and knead your dough if that's what you'd prefer. It is very satisfying working, kneading and creating your own dough but if you have your hands full already then use a machine. I am a mixer Mummy through and through. In a stand mixer work the ingredients together into a rough dough on speed setting 1. Then allow the machine to knead the dough for a full 10 minutes on setting 2. As it kneads, the dough hook should be slapping the dough around the bowl. If you are using a bread machine refer to the manufacturer's instructions. Be sure to keep an eye on your mixer as it kneads the dough: it could start to move across the work surface and you don't want it to take a tumble. If you're not able to watch it set it on the floor.

FIRST PROVING OR RISING

When the dough has been fully kneaded it is ready for the first proving or rising. Place 1 tsp sunflower or vegetable oil in the bottom of a bowl large enough to hold the dough when it has doubled in size. I prefer not to use a huge bowl as it can be difficult to judge when the dough has risen sufficiently.

Gather the dough together into a ball and place it in the bowl, turning it to coat the dough fully in the oil. Doing this means that it won't stick to the dish towel or cling film (plastic wrap) that is used to cover it.

The bowl should then be covered with a clean dish towel, cling film or, if you have a one, a clean, dry, disposable shower cap – the elasticated edge holds on to the bowl and they are big enough to stretch over most rims.

The dough should then be set somewhere at normal room temperature, away from any draughts, and be left to rise until doubled in volume. The yeast multiplies and as it does so releases carbon dioxide, which causes the rise. Warmth from a pre-heating oven or in an airing cupboard will encourage the dough to rise more quickly but it is not essential.

Dough can be left to rise overnight in the fridge for a slow, cool rise.

You will know when the dough is ready not only by sight – when it is touched with a finger it won't instantly spring back. Some doughs will take longer to reach this point and being patient is the key: don't rush your dough to the next stage before it is ready. Certain dough ingredients such as seeds, spices, malt extract and cocoa powder will slow down the speed at which a dough doubles in size at this stage.

KNOCKING BACK

After doubling in size the dough should be knocked back. This smoothes out any large air pockets and will give your bread an even texture. Simply punch the dough in the bowl to deflate it, turn it out onto the work surface and knead briefly, 1–2 minutes is usually sufficient.

If the recipe calls for them, any additions to the dough should be done at this point – you can easily do the working in and knocking back at the same time. Turn the dough out onto the work surface and stretch it out, scatter over the additions, gather up the dough and knead lightly to knock it back and incorporate the extra ingredients simultaneously. Now the dough is ready for shaping.

SHAPING DOUGH

Shaping creates the finished look of your loaf and is important for achieving an even rise.

Creating a spine and shaping a loaf

Dough needs a 'spine' so that the loaf will rise upwards rather than flowing outwards. This is especially important for free-form loaves. Flatten out the dough on the work surface into a rough round, for a round free-form loaf, or rectangle for a tin (pan) loaf **(1)**.

Take the edge of the dough and fold it in to the centre.**(2)** Continue all the way around the edge of the dough, folding in to the centre **(3)**. Repeat the process again, working around the dough, folding in to the middle until the dough is tightened and you can't fold in any more.

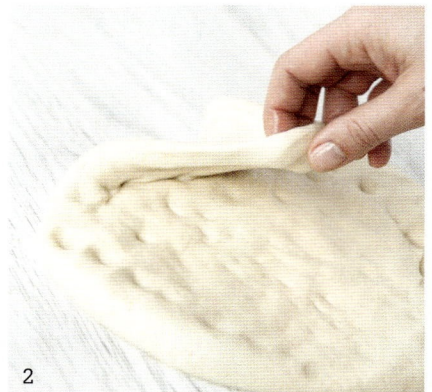

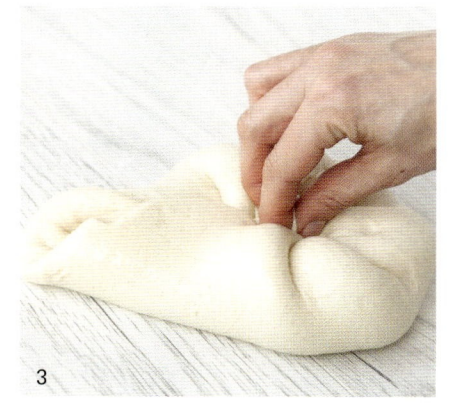

Flip the dough over on the work surface so that the seam sits underneath. Gently cup your hands around the ball of dough **(4)** (or either side of the loaf shape) and start to tighten the dough again, moving your hands down and underneath it **(5)**, repeating until the dough feels tightened like a coiled spring. Use your hands to shape the tightened dough into the required shape for a loaf tin (pan) or for a tapered free-form loaf. Your shaped dough now needs to be transferred to a greased loaf tin (pan) or a lined or well-greased baking sheet for its second proving.

To form rolls
Portion the dough evenly, flatten each portion and form a spine as described previously. Turn the dough over so that the seam sits underneath. Use your hand to form a cage around the ball of dough, with your fingertips firmly in contact with the work surface. Use your fingers to spin the dough, keeping your wrist elevated and allowing the dough to turn and tighten below your palm. Lift away your hand and there – a perfect roll!

For long rolls, form the spine and then a ball. Roll the ball between the palm of your hand and the work surface, applying an even pressure to create a sausage shape. To lengthen further, use two hands meeting together in the middle, and as you roll move your hands outwards to make the dough shape even longer. To taper the ends apply a greater pressure to the outside edge of both hands.

To shape a loaf in a proving basket/colander
Loaves shaped this way still need a spine. They are then placed into a well-floured proving basket (which can be expensive and only available from specialist shops). Lining a colander or large sieve with a cotton dish towel will provide the same result. Dust the dish towel well with flour before adding the shaped dough with the base facing upwards. When the loaf has doubled in size invert it onto a lined or greased baking sheet and remove the basket/colander and dish towel.

SECOND PROVING OR RISING
After shaping your loaf the dough should be allowed to prove or rise for a second time. It needs to be covered to prevent the dough from drying out, either with a clean dish towel or a sheet of thin plastic. An opened-out freezer bag is useful for covering baking sheets; loaves in tins (pans) can be loosely covered with cling film (plastic wrap) or a clean disposable shower cap. Shaped dough should be allowed to get to 85–90 per cent increased in size, which is why it's referred to in recipes as 'almost doubled

in size'. The heat from the oven gives some final oomph and makes the dough rise upwards in a last satisfying burst. The second proving is quicker than the first rise and (for regular doughs) should take 30–60 minutes. Getting this second rise is an important stage. Take care not to over-prove your dough or the loaf may collapse on baking. Under-proving can cause the top crust to balloon up and away from the bread leaving you with a gaping hole when sliced.

SLASHING LOAVES

Not only does slashing a loaf look attractive, it helps the dough to expand on baking. It needs to be done with a confident hand and a very sharp knife or razor blade. Hold the knife at a 45-degree angle to the surface of the dough, and don't press down but draw the blade across the dough instead. Loaves can be slashed prior to the second rise or just before baking. The earlier it's done then the wider the split will be. Just remember: super sharp and a swift, smooth, confident action. Flour the top of a loaf before slashing for more distinctive changes in appearance.

GLAZING BREAD

This will change the finished look of your bread and can be done with beaten egg (egg wash), milk, water, melted butter or warmed honey – to name but a few. For the best effect glaze should be gently brushed on just before baking. It also serves to give any sprinkled additions such as oats, chopped nuts or malted wheat flakes something to stick to.

BAKING

Getting to know how your oven bakes bread is just as important as your bread making technique. If you're in any doubt use a separate oven thermometer to test the accuracy of your oven's in-built thermometer. Preheat the oven with the thermometer on the shelf you will bake on, then adjust the oven temperature dial until the thermometer reads the correct temperature for your recipe. You should then be guaranteed correct baking times.

Every oven will bake good bread for you, but a fan oven can often darken the crust too much, so if you have the option

I would recommend setting your fan oven to the top and bottom heat only with no fan assistance and using the non-fan temperatures in the recipes. Be aware of the hot spots in your oven and consider positioning a shelf at the very top of the oven and adding an empty baking sheet to it at the same time as you put your loaf in to bake. The sheet will conduct the heat evenly over the top of your loaf and prevent it from scorching on the top.

Loaves get the last oomph of rising in the oven before the yeast is killed – which happens usually 10 minutes in to the baking time, so avoid opening the oven in this first stage of baking.

A falling temperature is most suitable for baking bread, using the initial burst of heat for the last rise and then a lower temperature to prevent browning too much before the bread is baked through. Adding the loaf to the oven will of course cause the temperature to fall a little – but in some recipes the oven temperature must be turned down after a certain amount of initial baking time.

The sugar in sweet doughs will create a darker crust and you should keep an eye on these from half way through baking onwards so that you can cover them with baking (parchment) paper if they appear to be browning too much.

Is it done?

Baking several loaves at the same time will increase the baking time as the load on the oven will increase and you will need to put your testing skills into action.

A fully baked loaf should sound hollow when tapped on the base. If the loaf is in a tin (pan) you will need to turn it out carefully to test it. If the sound is dull return the loaf to the oven for a further five minutes and test again.

A thermometer probe (used for testing the temperature of meat and other cooked foods) is extremely useful for checking whether bread is fully baked. If you have one put it into use and insert the probe, through the side, into the centre of the loaf – a fully baked loaf should read between 92–95°C/198–203°F.

AFTER BAKING

Bread should be turned out of the tin (pan) or transferred from the tray to a wire rack to cool straight away to prevent it from sweating.

Bread will always be best eaten freshly baked, on the day it has been made. It should be consumed within 1–2 days (2–3 days for breads with a high sugar or fat content) as it quickly goes stale without the preservatives that factories put into commercially produced bread.

You can refresh a whole loaf in the oven at 170°C/150°C (fan)/300°F/Gas mark 2 for 15 minutes to restore it almost to the quality of 'just baked'.

Loaves should be stored in a cool, dry bread bin, not the fridge. Wrap in a plastic bag for a soft crust and baking (parchment) paper or a paper bag for crusty bread.

Home-baked bread freezes well for up to a month in a freezer bag, but consider slicing/portioning the loaf so you can defrost just as much as you need. Defrost at room temperature and then refresh in the oven as above.

EXTRA CRUSTY

If you like it super crusty, preheat a roasting tin (pan) in the base of the oven. As soon as you add your loaf to the oven to bake add a cup of cold water to the hot tin and close the oven door. This creates a hot, steamy oven that will give you an even crisper crust.

TROUBLESHOOTING

My dough won't rise!
First of all did you add the yeast? It's an obvious suggestion but it does happen! If the dough is cold then the yeast will take longer to create the rise, so you need to allow more time. If you don't have time to wait for the required rise then you can warm up the dough to get it going. Try a warmer position – maybe next to a preheating oven or in an airing cupboard. You could set the dough on a tray over a large bowl filled with a little hot water: the dough will absorb the warmth which should get it springing into action.

My loaf is doughy in texture
The problem here is that the loaf has not baked through fully, and the moisture still in the loaf will cause it to have a doughy texture. Under baking can also cause the crust to soften and the loaf to sag. Double check the oven for temperature accuracy with an oven thermometer.

My loaf has collapsed/looks saggy
If dough is over-proved it can collapse in the oven while baking as it doesn't have the structure to hold itself up. On second proving only allow your loaf to rise to 85–90 per cent, leaving the last small percentage of rise to happen in the oven.

My loaf has big holes underneath the crust/a tight seam of dough at the base/is dense in texture
These problems are caused by under proving a loaf before baking. Make sure that the dough has swelled to 85–90 per cent of its original size before baking otherwise the crust can fly upwards in a balloon effect, separating from the dough, and leaving a gaping hole between the crust and the loaf. It is also the cause of a seam of what looks like uncooked dough in the bottom 5mm (¼ in) of a loaf and will leave you with dense-textured bread.

My free-form loaf hasn't risen upwards and is wide and shallow instead...
This is down to the dough having an insufficient spine to give it enough structure to rise upwards. Work at creating a strong spine on the next loaf you make which will stop it from flowing outwards.

My loaf has split
This can be down to two things – under proving or the oven being too hot. Be sure to preheat the oven to the right temperature and position the loaf in the centre of the oven, away from the door and sides which will conduct heat and create hot spots.

My loaf is burnt on top
Sweet bread may need covering with baking (parchment) paper after half the baking time if it appears to be browning too much on top – the sugar in the dough will create a darker crust. If the top of the oven is creating uneven hot spots position a shelf in the very top of the oven and add a baking sheet to it at the same time as adding your loaf to bake. It will heat up gradually with the loaf and conduct heat evenly onto the top of the loaf, helping to prevent it from burning.

My loaf is burnt on the bottom
The base of an oven can also conduct heat unevenly and scorch the base of a loaf. Try setting the loaf tin, or baking sheet that a free-form loaf is sitting on, on top of another baking sheet before placing onto the oven shelf to bake. This will help to stop the base from burning.

My loaf has a wrinkly crust
If a loaf is deeply wrinkled then the dough has been underproved before baking. If the crust is a little wrinkled but was smooth when it first came out of the oven then this is due to it cooling too quickly on the rack in a draught. Loaves with a thin, fine crust will often be prone to this as the bread contracts as it cools.

My loaf has a cakey texture
A cakey texture is produced when dough hasn't been kneaded enough. The gluten hasn't been developed and stretched enough to create the proper bread texture you expect in a loaf.

BRILLIANT BASICS

These recipes are the straightforward ones, and if you're new to bread making this is where you need to be. They are a great introduction and practising them will mean you get to know the techniques involved and consistencies needed to produce a great loaf. Highly satisfying too – there'll be bread on your table in next to no time.

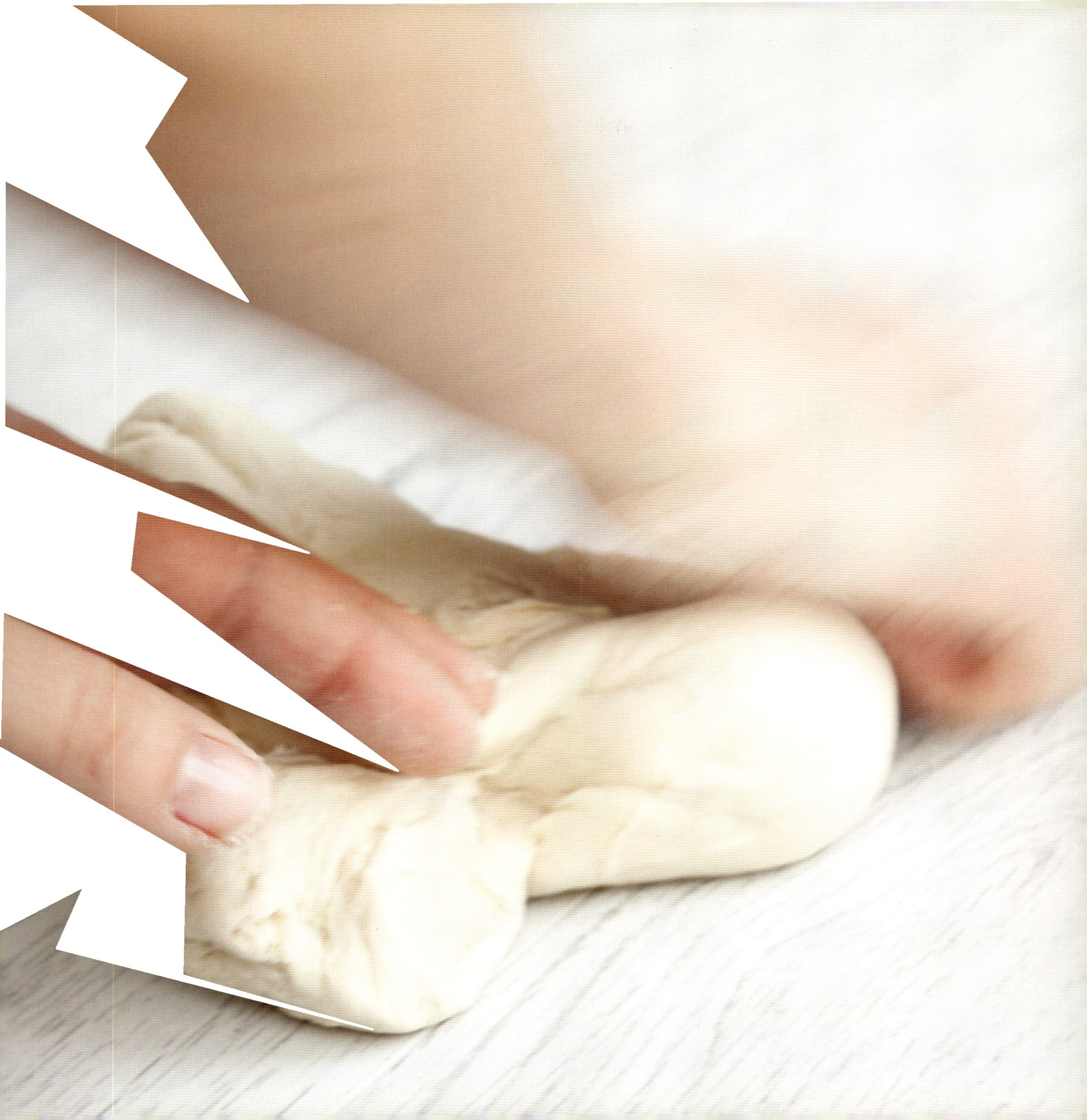

BASIC WHITE LOAF

MAKES ONE 900G (2LB) LOAF
PREP ⏲ 30 MINUTES PLUS 1½ HOURS PROVING
BAKE ⏲ 35 MINUTES | OVEN 190°C (FAN)/210°C/425°F/GAS MARK 7

A straightforward white loaf is up first, and probably the best place to start if you're new to bread making. Perfect for sandwiches, popping in the toaster or dunking in a bowl of soup.

INGREDIENTS

Bread

400g (14oz) strong white bread flour

2 tsp fast action yeast

1 tsp caster (superfine) sugar

1 tsp salt

170ml/170g (6fl oz/6oz) water

83 ml/85g (2¾fl oz/3oz) milk

EQUIPMENT

900g (2lb) loaf tin

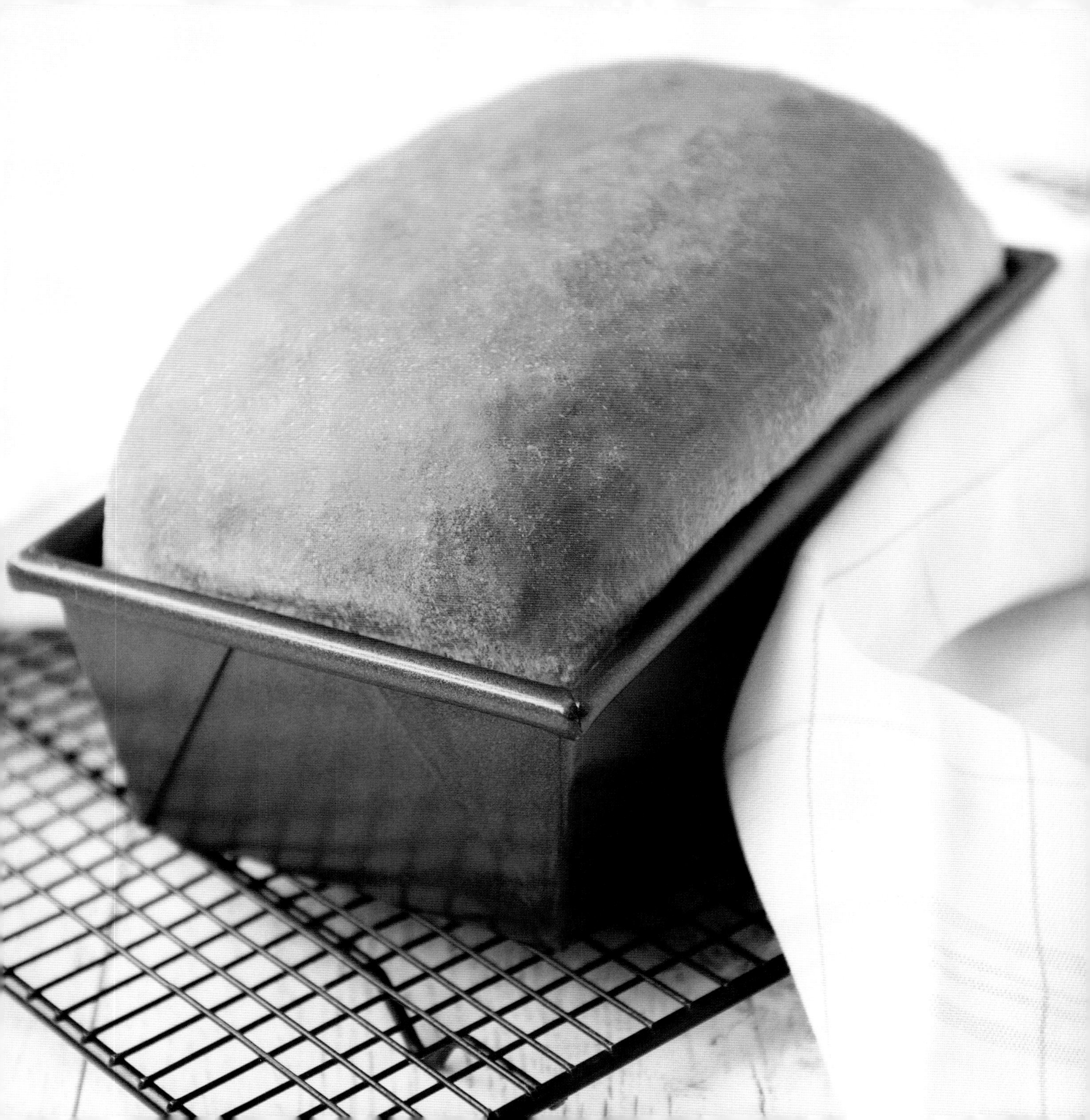

1. First measure the flour into a large mixing bowl. Add in the yeast, sugar and salt, placing each in a different part of the flour. It's best to avoid the salt touching the yeast at this stage as it can inhibit its effectiveness.

2. Now for the water and milk. The liquid for dough shouldn't be cold, but lukewarm – this springs the yeast straight into action. You can warm the liquid through in the microwave but it also works well to measure the water hot from the kettle and then add the milk cold from the fridge. Set to one side.

3. Stir together the dry ingredients: you're going to have to get your hands in at some point so it might as well be now! Once the yeast, salt and sugar are fairly evenly distributed make a well in the centre and pour in the water/ milk mixture.

4. Using your fingers start to work the dry ingredients into the wet. Keep working until it forms a shaggy dough with everything incorporated.

Brilliant Basics

5 Turn the dough out onto the work surface. Don't be tempted to add any extra flour to the surface as this would be incorporated into the dough as you knead and toughen the finished bread. It may seem sticky to begin with but persevere. Using both hands knead the dough for ten minutes. Stretch the dough away from you then pull it back onto itself, repeating the action with both hands and allowing the dough to turn as you knead it.

6 After five minutes of kneading the dough will be much more elastic and will look a lot less shaggy.

7 After 10 minutes the dough will be far smoother, non-sticky and ready to prove. 10 minutes of kneading is fairly hard work, certainly for your arms, but it is essential. Set a timer and be strict with yourself not to be distracted. You can reward yourself with a cup of tea when the timer goes off!

8 Now prepare a bowl for the dough to rest in. Not so large that it's rattling around on its lonesome; a smaller bowl will keep the dough snug and draught free – a 1.5l (1½ US quart) capacity is ideal. Grease the base and sides of the bowl with a teaspoon of sunflower or vegetable oil and pop the dough in, then turn it to give it a very light coating of the oil.

Basic White Loaf **25**

9 Cover with cling film (plastic wrap) or a clean dish towel and set somewhere at room temperature away from draughts and direct sunlight. Leave to rise for 1 hour or until doubled in size. If it's kept somewhere cool it will take longer to double: be patient, this stage is important. Using a smaller bowl makes it easier to see when the dough has doubled – in a large bowl this can be deceiving.

10 Once doubled in size, tip the dough out onto your work surface. Again, no flour is needed. Gently knead the dough for a couple of minutes; this knocks it back and deflates it. It should be much, much softer and more elastic than before.

11 Flatten the dough out into a rough rectangle. Take hold of the edge of the dough and fold it in to the centre. Work your way all around the dough folding in to the centre leaving you with a smaller-shaped piece of dough. Repeat the folding in to the centre again, tightening the dough until you can fold into the middle no more – this creates a spine for the loaf and will ensure an even rise.

12 Flip the dough over so that the seam is underneath. Cup your hands with thumbs touching around the top of the dough, then slide your hands down the sides and underneath the dough in a tightening action. Repeat the tightening action, gently encouraging the dough to shape into the rough length of your tin, all the time keeping the seam underneath.

Brilliant Basics

13 Grease the loaf tin and pop in the shaped dough. Give it a light dusting of flour if you like. Cover it again loosely with cling film (plastic wrap) or clean dish towel and put it in the same draught-free spot as the first proving for its final rise. 30 minutes should be sufficient, so preheat the oven to 190°C (fan)/210°C/425°F/Gas Mark 7.

14 The dough will have almost doubled in size. Almost is the key here: it should be domed over the top of the tin. You need to leave some room for oven spring – the last burst of rise when the loaf goes into the oven. If the dough is left too long at this stage the dough becomes over-proved – the yeast loses its power and can leave you with a very wrinkled crust. Remove the cling film (plastic wrap) or dish towel and put the loaf straight into the middle of the oven, quickly, and shut the door, to keep in as much of the heat as possible. Bake for 35 minutes.

15 When removing from the oven, turn the loaf out of the tin (pan) as soon as possible. If left in it will sweat and the moisture will be reabsorbed by the loaf leaving you with soggy bread! When fully baked the base of the loaf when tapped should sound hollow. If there is a dull sound then it needs more time in the oven to bake through fully. If it sounds nice and hollow transfer it to a wire rack to cool.

Basic White Loaf **27**

BASIC BROWN LOAF

It's great to have a basic wholemeal (whole wheat) bread recipe in your repertoire but it's not just as simple as replacing white flour with brown. Wholemeal (whole wheat) flour absorbs much more liquid than white and can produce a very dense loaf. This basic loaf is made with a combination of flours to give a much nicer texture.

MAKES ONE 900G (2LB) LOAF
PREP 30 MINUTES PLUS 1½ HOURS PROVING
BAKE 35 MINUTES
OVEN 190°C (FAN)/210°C/425°F/GAS MARK 7

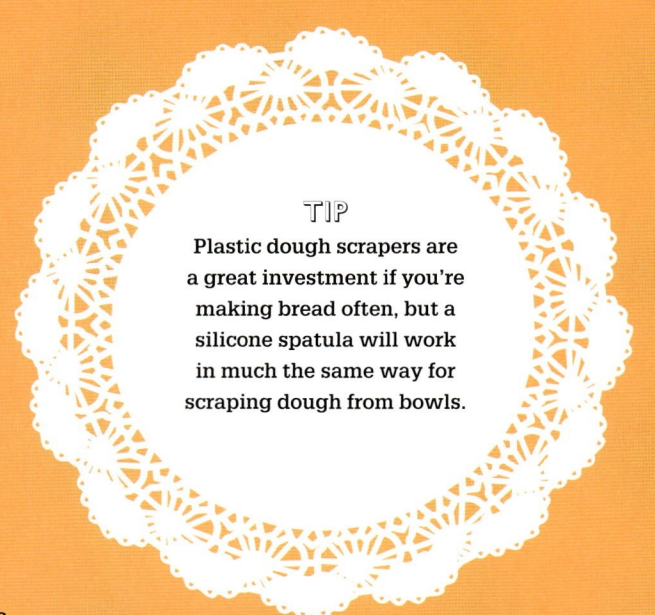

INGREDIENTS
Bread
160g (5¾oz) strong white bread flour
240g (8½oz) strong wholemeal (whole-wheat) bread flour
2 tsp fast action yeast
1 tsp caster (superfine) sugar
1 tsp salt
220ml/220g (7¾fl oz /7¾oz) water
49ml/50g (1¾fl oz/1¾oz) milk

Equipment
900g (2lb) loaf tin

Follow the same method as the Basic White Loaf but use a combination of wholemeal (whole wheat) and white flours and a slightly increased amount of liquid.

TIP
Plastic dough scrapers are a great investment if you're making bread often, but a silicone spatula will work in much the same way for scraping dough from bowls.

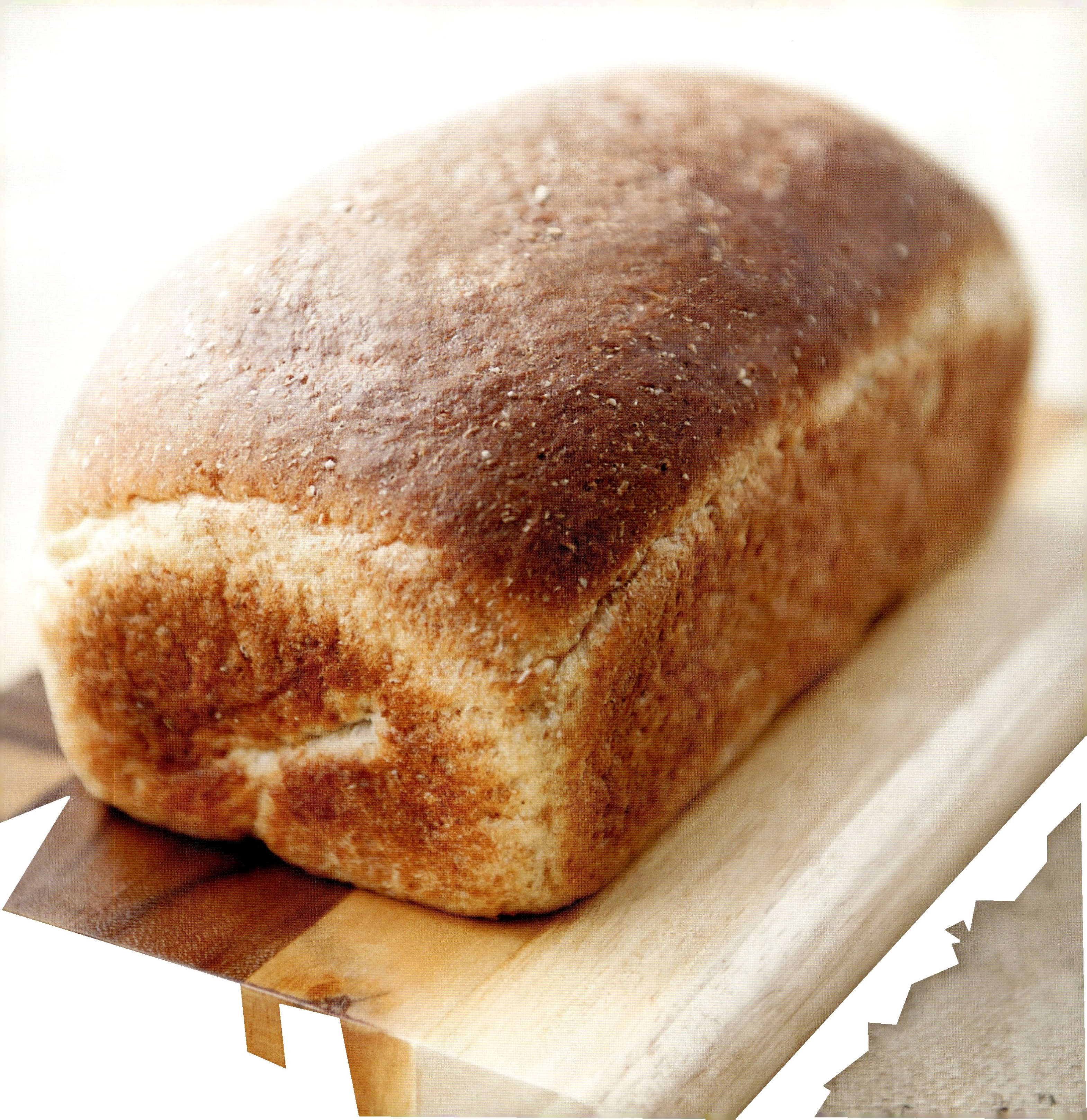

QUICK WHITE ROLLS

MAKES 8 ROLLS
PREP ⏲ **20 MINUTES PLUS 30 MINUTES PROVING**
BAKE ⏲ **15 MINUTES | OVEN 190°C (FAN)/210°C/425°F/GAS MARK 7**

This is a quick-fix bread recipe, perfect when you've run out of bread and need some on the double! Defying all the long, slow rules of bread making, these are similar in texture to traditional English oven-bottom muffins and are just as good for a lunchtime sandwich as they are for dunking in a bowl of steaming hearty soup. You can easily go from no bread to freshly baked rolls in just about an hour.

INGREDIENTS

425g (15oz) strong white bread flour
1 tsp caster (superfine) sugar
1 tsp salt
3 tsp fast action yeast
50g (1¾oz) butter, diced and softened
240ml/240g (9oz/9fl oz) water, lukewarm
Oil for greasing

EQUIPMENT

Rolling pin
Baking sheet

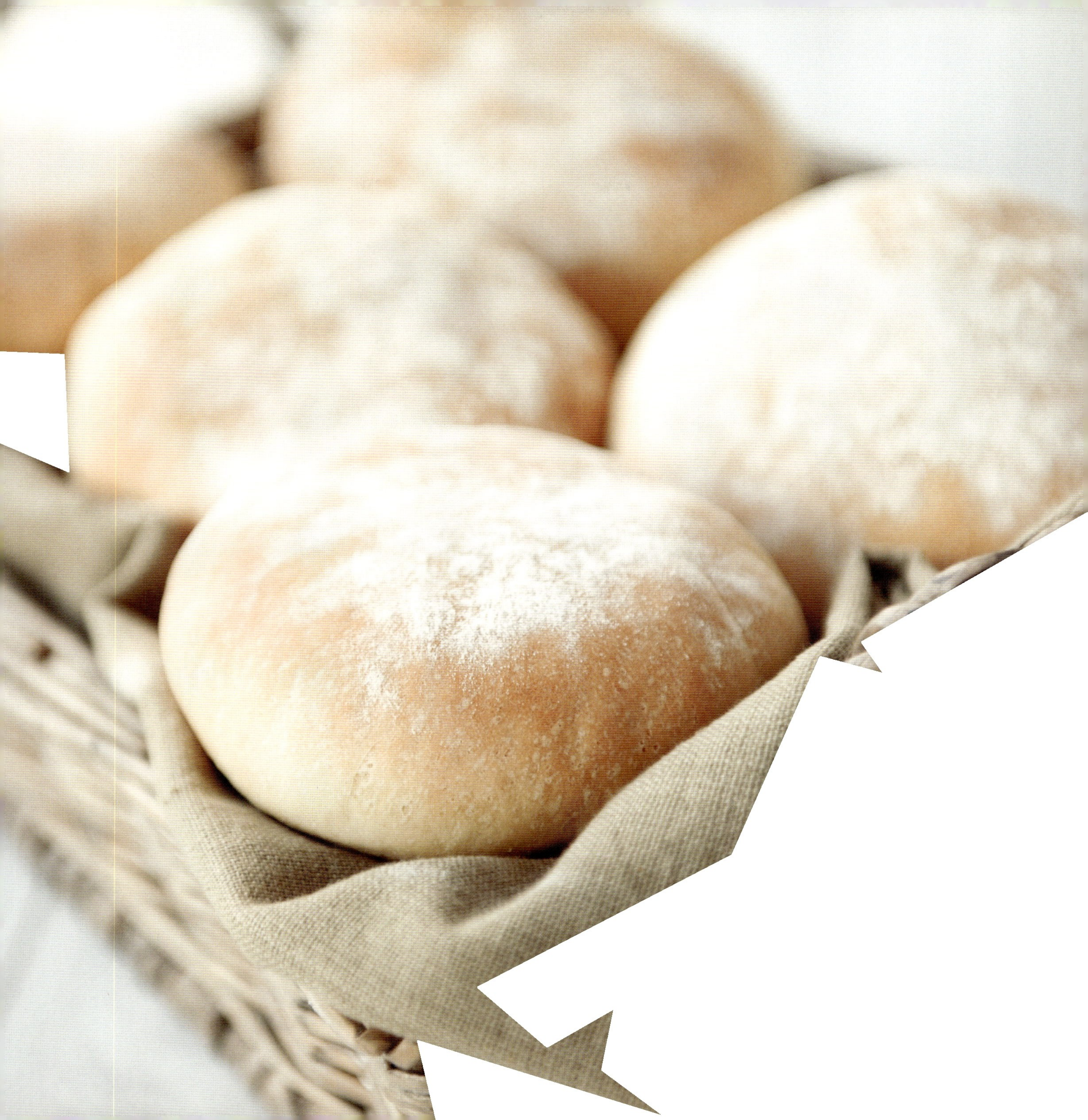

1 Preheat the oven to 190°C (fan)/210°C/425°F/Gas Mark 7: this will start to warm up the kitchen and get these super quick rolls jumping into action. Place all the dry ingredients into a large mixing bowl and add the diced, softened butter.

TIP

The butter should be room temperature so that it can be easily incorporated into the dough. Too cold and it will be difficult to mix in and will also lower the temperature of the dough. Speed is of the essence so maintaining a warm dough temperature is important.

2 Warm the water so it is lukewarm. The warmth is needed to spring the yeast into action and get these rolls on the go as soon as possible. Pour the warm water into the bowl and mix everything together to form a rough dough.

3 Knead the dough for ten minutes until smooth and elastic. Add a teaspoon of vegetable or sunflower oil to a clean mixing bowl. Transfer the ball of dough to the bowl and turn to coat in the oil.

4 Cover the bowl with cling film (plastic wrap) or a clean dish towel and place in a warm spot, ideally near to the preheating oven, and allow to rest for 15 minutes. After resting the dough will have already started to puff up a little.

32 Brilliant Basics

5 Instead of knocking back the dough as you would with a regular loaf simply turn it out onto your work surface and divide it into 8 equal portions of approximately 90g (3¼oz) each. The dividing and shaping will knock back the dough. Taking one portion of dough at a time, use your hand to form a cage around each ball of dough, with your fingertips in contact with the work surface. Use your fingers to gently spin the dough, keeping your wrist elevated and allowing the dough to turn and tighten below your palm until the dough forms a nice neat ball.

6 Gently press out each ball with a rolling pin, just a couple of light rolls forwards and backwards and then left to right will do the trick. Your finished roll should be about 8cm (3¼in) in diameter. Transfer the rolls to a well greased or lined baking sheet, spaced well enough apart to allow for a little spreading. Dust the tops of the rolls with flour and cover with a clean dish towel. Now back into the warm spot to rise for 15 minutes.

TIP Using a rolling pin helps to keep an even round shape, but for speed the rolls could be pressed out lightly with the palm of your hand.

7 After 15 minutes they should be a little puffy – far from the usual second rise but these are good to go! Straight into the preheated oven with them for 15 minutes.

8 Once baked remove from the oven and transfer gently to a wire rack to cool completely. The tops will feel like they have a hard crust but will soon soften up on cooling. Now go dunk them in your soup!

TEA CAKES

Just as super quick as the white rolls, you'll be toasting and buttering these delicious teacakes in next to no time.

MAKES 8 LARGE TEACAKES
PREP 🕐 25 MINUTES PLUS 30 MINUTES PROVING
BAKE 🕐 15 MINUTES
OVEN 190°C (FAN)/210°C/425° F/GAS MARK 7

INGREDIENTS

425g (15oz) strong white bread flour
30g (1oz) caster (superfine) sugar
1 tsp salt
3 tsp fast action yeast
100g (3½oz) raisins
50g (1¾oz) butter, diced and softened
240ml/240g (9oz/9fl oz) water, lukewarm
Oil for greasing

EQUIPMENT

Rolling pin
Baking sheet

Use exactly the same method for the quick white rolls but increase the caster (superfine) sugar to 30g (1oz) and add 100g (3½oz) raisins to the dry ingredients when mixing up the dough.

TIP

When it comes to dividing the dough into 8, the individual weight of each teacake is approximately 105g (3¾oz).

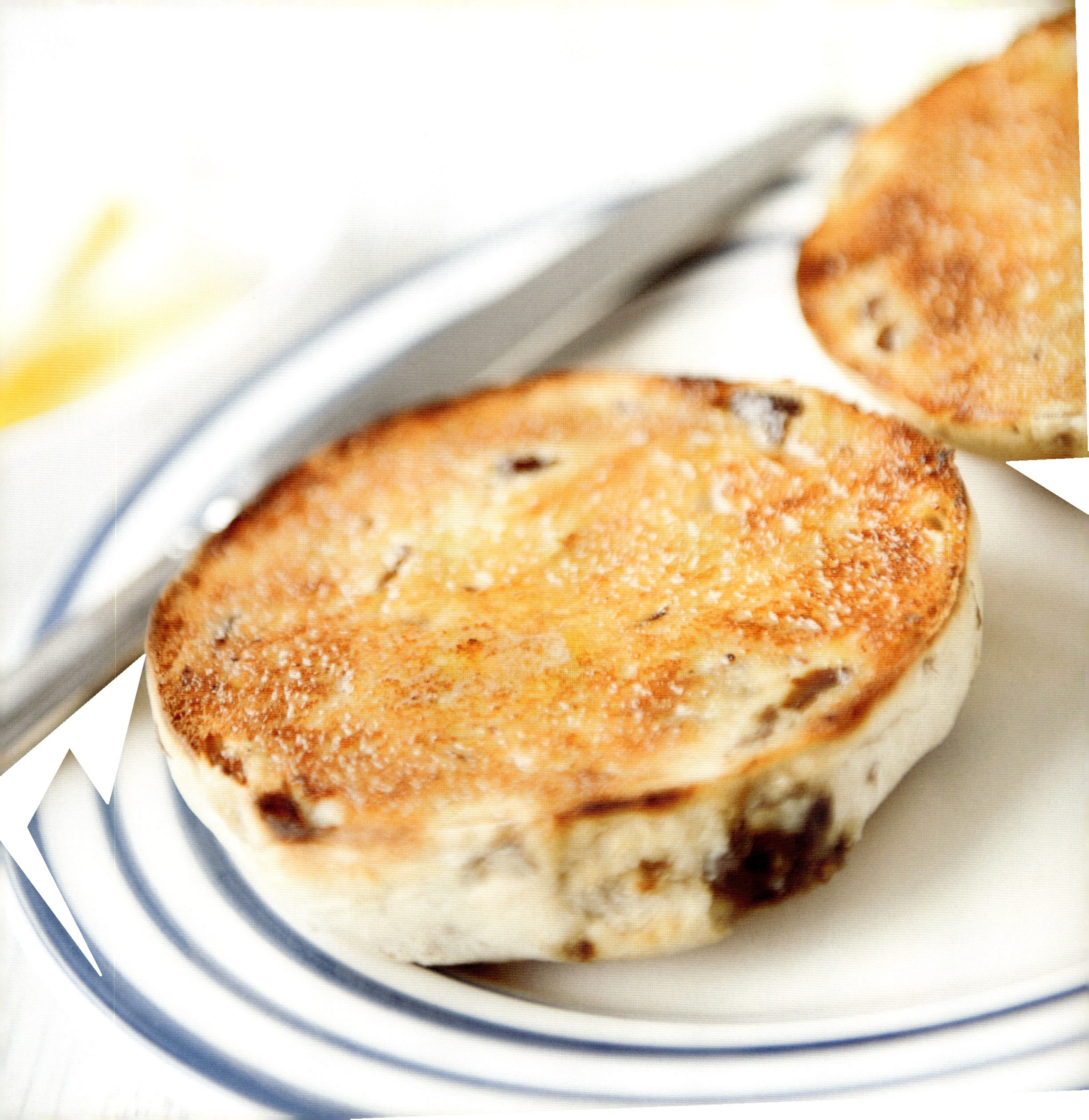

BBQ TWIST & SWIRL LOAF

MAKES 1 LARGE TIN (PAN) LOAF
PREP 🕐 **25 MINUTES PLUS 2 HOURS 10 MINUTES PROVING**
BAKE 🕐 **30 MINUTES | OVEN 190°C (FAN)/210°C/425°F/GAS MARK 7**

A twisted white loaf hiding tangy BBQ swirls inside. It's extremely easy to do and certainly has the wow factor when you slice it open! It's important not to under-prove this loaf and to ensure you roll tightly otherwise the swirls won't be tight and the bread will have lots of holes between the swirls.

INGREDIENTS

Bread
300g (10½oz) strong white bread flour
¾ tsp salt
¾ tsp caster (superfine) sugar
1½ tsp fast action yeast
185ml/190g (6½fl oz/6¾oz) milk
4 tsp vegetable or sunflower oil
Oil for greasing

Filling
3 tbsp BBQ marinade
Milk to glaze

EQUIPMENT
900g (2lb) loaf tin (pan)
Pastry brush

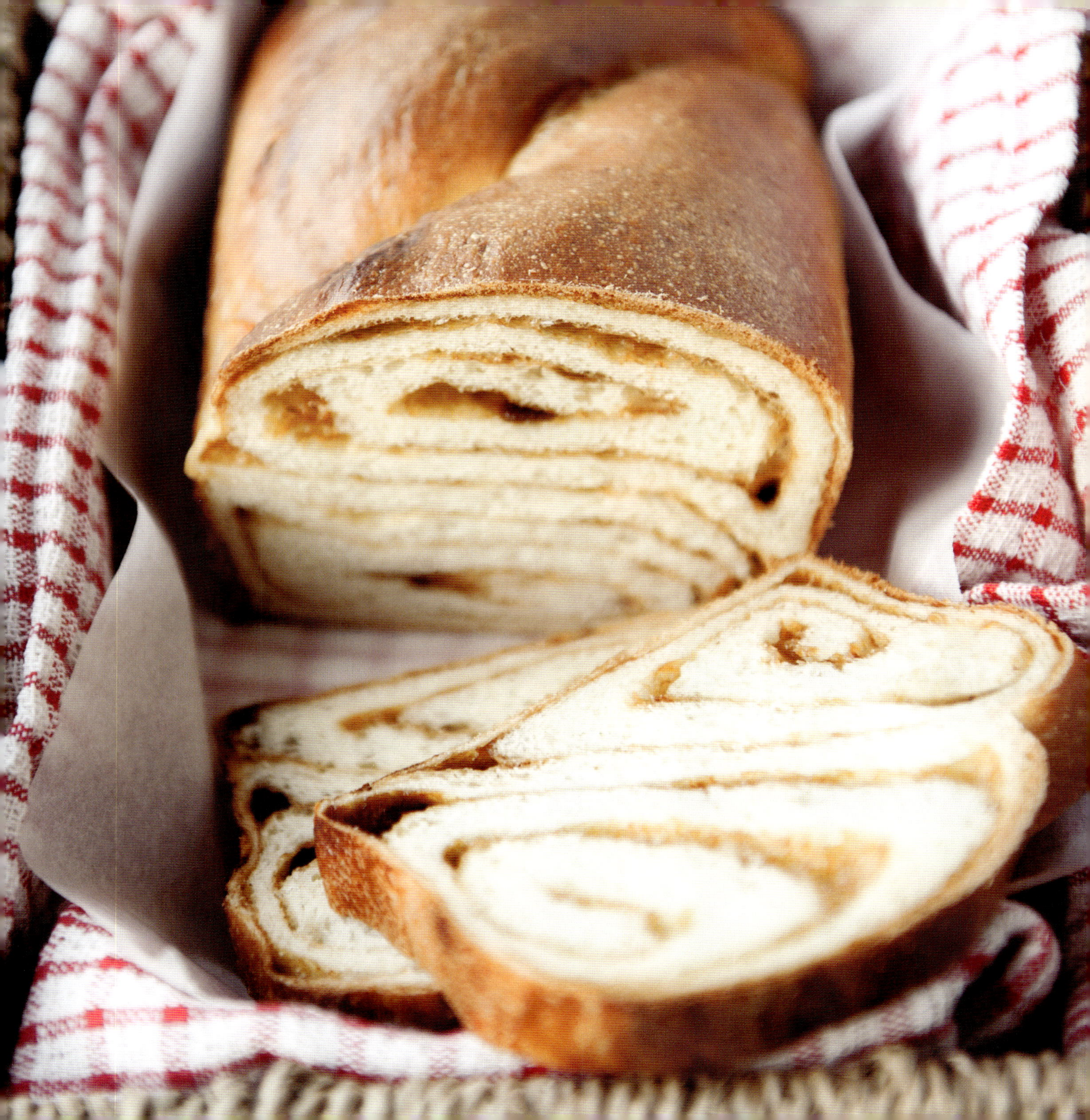

1. To make the dough combine the flour, salt, sugar and yeast. Warm the milk to a lukewarm temperature and add to the dry ingredients along with 4 tsp vegetable oil. Mix together to form a rough dough.

2. Turn the dough out onto the work surface and knead for 10 minutes until smooth. Place the dough in a lightly oiled bowl, turn it to coat and cover the bowl with cling film (plastic wrap). Place in a warm spot to rise for 1 hour or until doubled in size.

3. Turn the dough out onto your work surface and knead very lightly. Now using your hands gently stretch out the dough into a large rectangle, approximately 40 x 30cm (16 x 12in). The dough should be nice and elastic and stretch easily without tearing. If it's tearing it's not quite ready yet; leave it a little longer to rise before trying again.

4. Arrange the dough rectangle so that the longest edges are horizontal. Spread the BBQ marinade over the surface of the dough, aiming for an even covering and keeping it 2cm (¾in) away from the shorter sides and the long edge of the dough furthest from you.

TIP
Twist and swirl loaves can be filled with all sorts of flavourings: red or green pesto, curry pastes, even sundried tomatoes and fresh basil. Make up your own variations – there's only one way to find out if it will work and that's to give it a go!

38 Brilliant Basics

5 From the long edge nearest to you start to roll up the dough, nice and tightly, avoiding any air pockets if possible.

6 When you get to the end, pinch together the dough, along the length, to seal. Turn the roll so that the seam sits underneath. Pinch the ends together to seal in the swirl.

7 Fold the sausage of dough in the middle and wrap the two lengths around each other twice to create the twist. Tuck the ends underneath the loaf neatly and place it into a greased loaf tin (pan).

8 Cover and allow to rise for 30 minutes or until doubled in size. This is important: if the loaf goes into the oven under-proved then the top will balloon up leaving you with a hole just below the crust and holes through the uppermost swirls. Preheat the oven to 190°C (fan)/210°C/425°F/Gas Mark 7.

9 Brush the top with a little milk to glaze then bake in the preheated oven for 30 minutes. Transfer to a wire rack and allow to cool completely.

TIP If there's any left over this bread is fantastic for cheese on toast!

BBQ Twist & Swirl Loaf

CINNAMON TWIST & SWIRL LOAF

A sweet variation of the Twist & Swirl loaf with a warming injection of cinnamon.

MAKES 1 LARGE TIN (PAN) LOAF
PREP 25 MINUTES PLUS 2 HOURS 10 MINUTES PROVING
BAKE: 30 MINUTES
OVEN 190°C (FAN)/210°C/425°F/GAS MARK 7

TIP
Scatter over 100g (3½oz) raisins or sultanas (golden raisins) when adding the sugar/cinnamon mix to the stretched out dough to create a fruited version.

INGREDIENTS
Bread
300g (10½oz) strong white bread flour
½ tsp salt
20g (¾oz) caster (superfine) sugar
1½ tsp fast action yeast
1½ tsp cinnamon
185ml/190g (6½fl oz/6¾oz) milk, lukewarm
4 tsp vegetable or sunflower oil
Oil for greasing

Filling
40g (1½oz) dark muscovado sugar
1½ tsp cinnamon
Milk to glaze

EQUIPMENT
900g (2lb) loaf tin

1. Follow the recipe for the BBQ Twist & Swirl Loaf but increase the sugar in this dough to 20g (¾oz) and decrease the salt to just ½tsp to create a sweet dough. Add the ground cinnamon to the dry mixture and then mix as before.

2. When it comes to the filling, combine 40g dark muscovado sugar with 1½ tsp ground cinnamon and sprinkle over the stretched out dough.

3. Roll and twist as per the BBQ version, leave to rise until almost doubled in size, glaze with milk and bake in the preheated oven for 30 minutes.

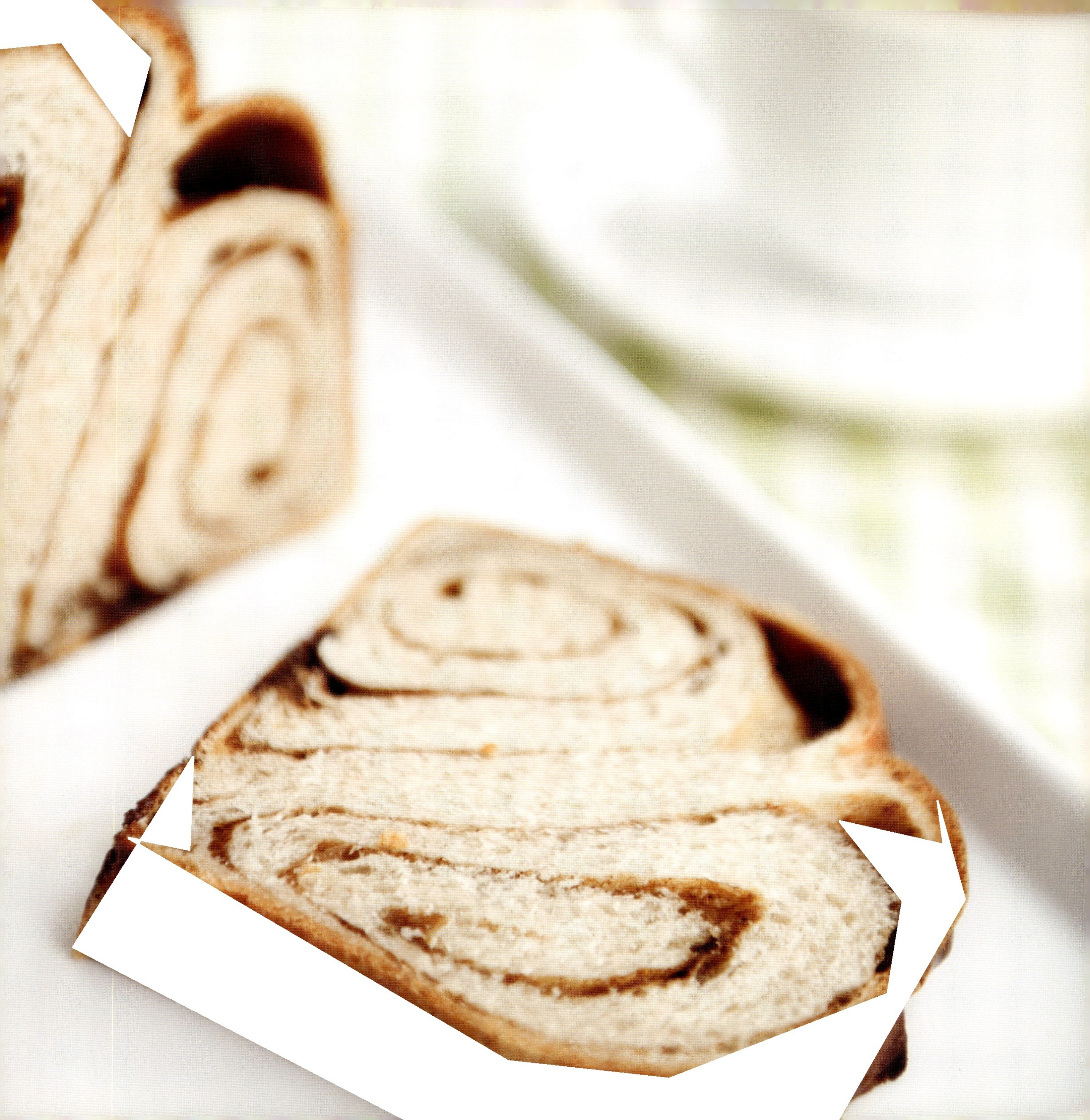

MALTHOUSE LOAF

MAKES 1 LARGE FREE-FORM LOAF
PREP ⏲ 20 MINUTES PLUS 2 HOURS 15 MINUTES PROVING
BAKE ⏲ 30 MINUTES | OVEN 190°C (FAN)/210°C/425°F/GAS MARK 7

A dark, grainy, malted bread – hearty and tasty. With a crisp crust and speckled with malted wheat flakes, this is definitely a show-stopper of a loaf.

INGREDIENTS
Bread
450g (1lb) strong malted grain bread flour
1 tsp salt
1 tsp caster (superfine) sugar
2 tsp fast action yeast
2 tbsp malt extract
235ml/235g (8½fl oz/8½oz) water, lukewarm

Topping
1 tbsp wheat flakes

EQUIPMENT
Pastry brush
Baking sheet

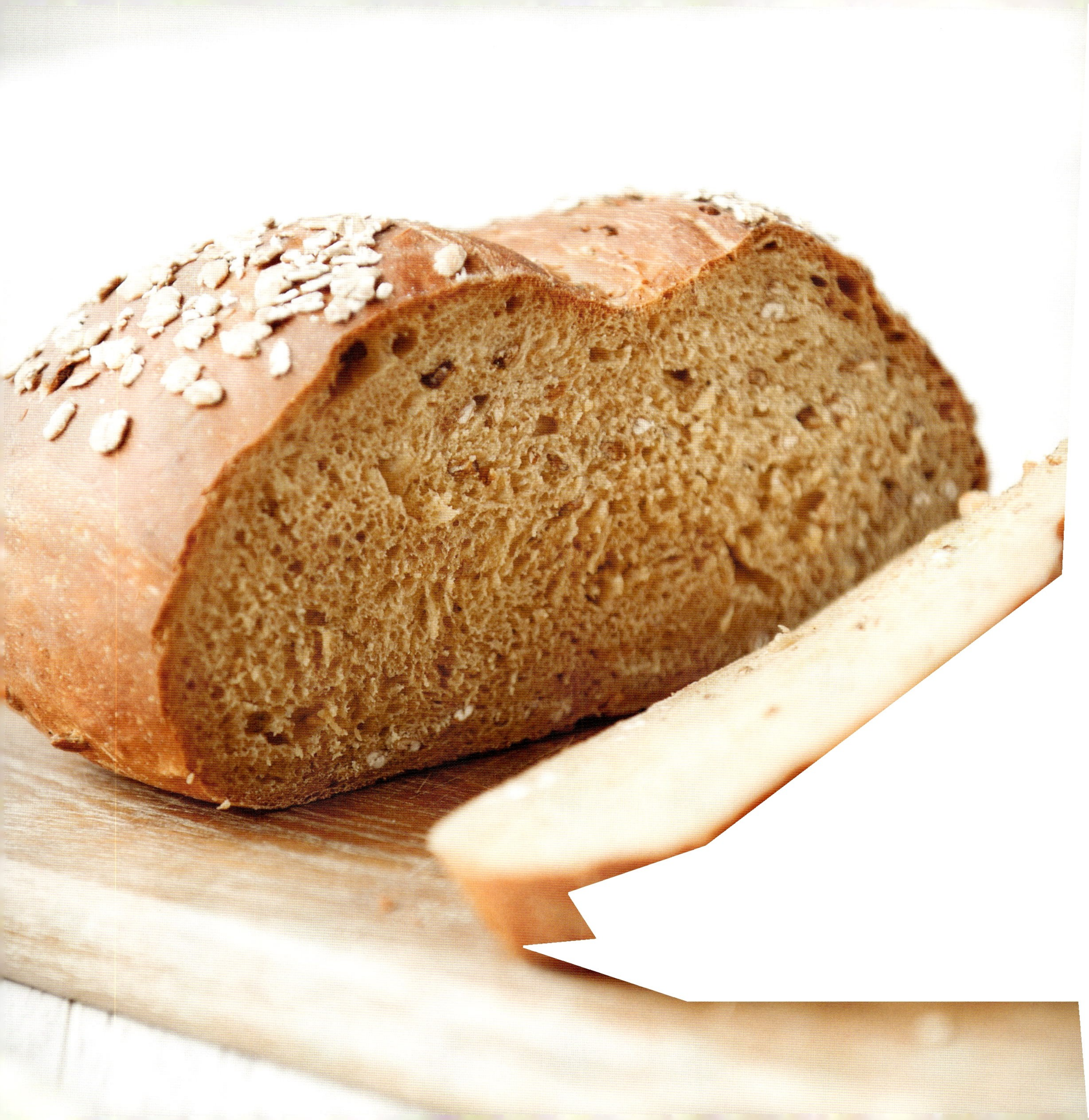

1. To make the dough place the flour, salt, sugar and yeast in a large mixing bowl and stir to combine. Make a well in the centre and add first the malt extract and then the water.

TIP
Greasing the tablespoon with a little vegetable oil will stop malt extract, treacle (molasses) or honey from sticking and the full measured amount will slide straight out into the recipe.

2. Mix together in the bowl to form a rough dough. Turn out onto the work surface and knead for 10 minutes until smooth. It will be a little sticky to begin with but will become less so when worked so keep going! Don't be tempted to add any extra flour to the work surface as this will toughen the dough and the finished loaf. If you really can't stand the stickiness grease your hands with a little vegetable oil.

3. Place the dough in a lightly oiled bowl, turn it to coat and cover with cling film (plastic wrap). Transfer to a warm, draught-free spot to rise for 1½ hours or until doubled in size.

4. Once doubled in size turn the dough out onto your work surface and knead briefly. Flatten out the dough and start to turn the edges in to the centre, working all the way around. Repeat the folding in until the dough is tightened into a rough ball.

44 Brilliant Basics

5 Flip the ball of dough over so that the seam is underneath. Shape the ball into an oval, gently tapering the ends.

TIP For any additions to stick to the top of a loaf it will need to be brushed with a little water or milk to give the wheat flakes/oats/seeds something to stick to. Additions or flour should be in place before slashing a loaf with a sharp knife so that the distinctive split is created.

6 Transfer the loaf to a lined or well greased baking sheet, gently brush the top of the loaf with a little water and scatter on the wheat flakes. Using a sharp knife or blade slash the top of the loaf from one tapered end to the other.

7 Cover with a clean dish towel and set back in the warm spot to rise for 45 minutes or until almost doubled in size. Preheat the oven to 190°C (fan)/210°C/425°F/Gas Mark 7.

TIP For the second rise the loaf should be allowed to get to almost doubled in size, you're aiming for 90 per cent – allowing for a 10 per cent burst once the loaf goes into the oven in the first hit of heat.

8 Bake in the preheated oven for 30 minutes. Transfer to a wire rack and allow to cool completely.

Malthouse Loaf 45

HONEY OAT ROLLS

A lighter version of the Malthouse Loaf with a hint of sweetness, but still packed with all the goodness of malthouse flour and rolled oats.

MAKES 8 ROLLS
PREP 25 MINUTES PLUS 1 HOUR 50 MINUTES PROVING
BAKE 15 MINUTES
OVEN 190°C (FAN)/210°C/425°F/GAS MARK 7

1. Follow the method in the Malthouse Loaf but decrease the flour to 425g (15oz) and add 55g (2oz) rolled oats. Combine with the salt, sugar and yeast before adding 2 tbsp honey and the water, mixing to form a dough.

2. After the first rising divide the dough into 8 equal-sized portions (approximately 92g (3¼oz) each) and roll into rough balls.

3. To shape the tapered rolls take a ball of dough and roll it back and forth across the work surface applying pressure with both hands – slightly more pressure to the outside edge of each hand will taper the ends to points. Each shaped roll should be approximately 14cm (5½in) in length.

4. Transfer to a lined baking sheet, brush the top of each with a little water and scatter over the additional rolled oats. Using a sharp knife slash the tops of the rolls from one tapered end to the other.

5. Cover with a dish towel to rise for 20 minutes or until nearly doubled in size, then bake in the preheated oven for 15 minutes.

INGREDIENTS
Bread
425g (15oz) strong malted grain bread flour
55g (2oz) rolled oats
1 tsp salt
1 tsp caster (superfine) sugar
2 tsp fast action yeast
2 tbsp runny honey
235ml/235g (8½fl oz/8½oz) water, lukewarm

Topping
2 tbsps rolled oats

EQUIPMENT
Pastry brush
Baking sheet

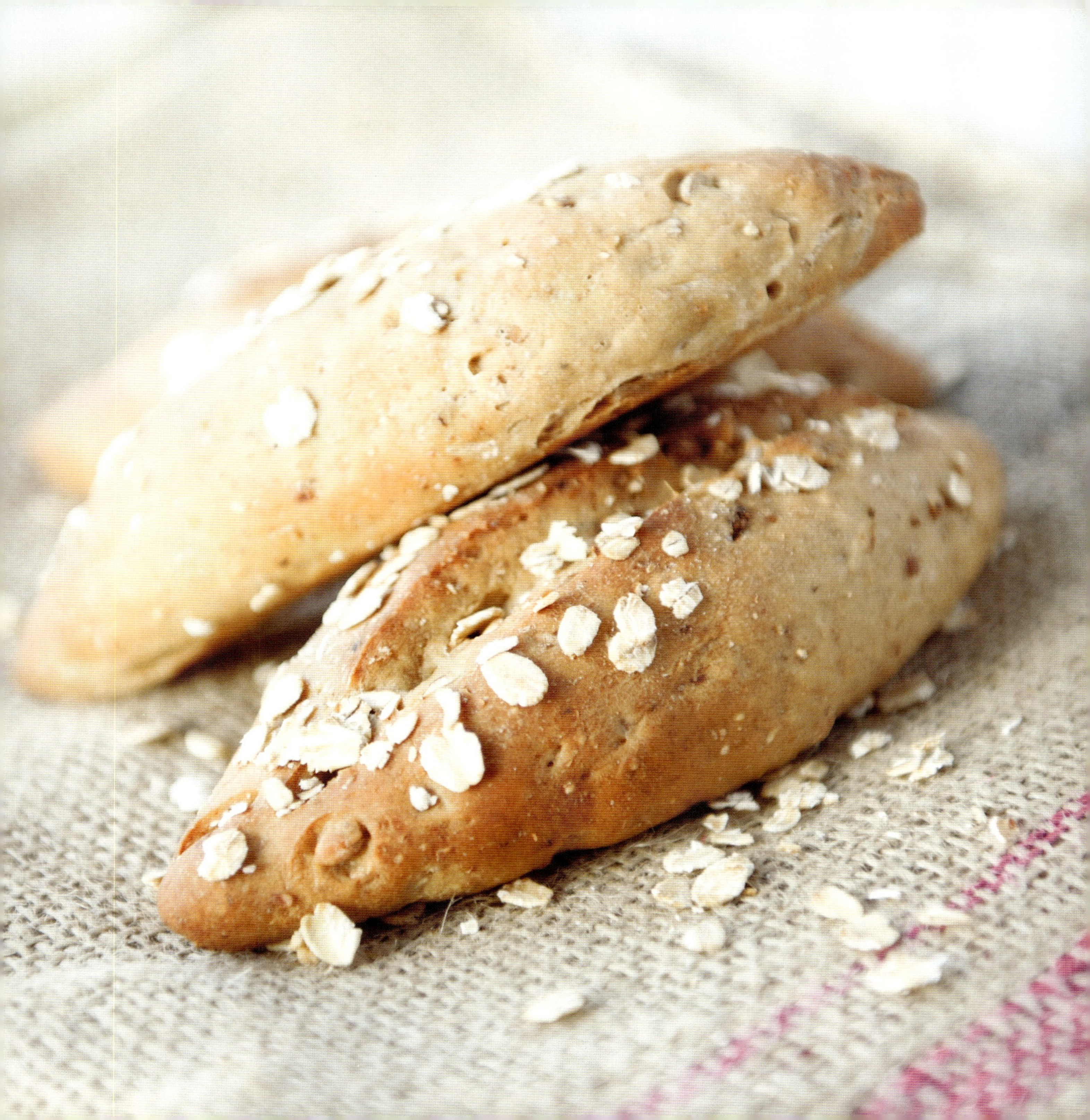

BACON & CHEESE POTATO BREAD

MAKES 1 ROUND LOAF
PREP 🕐 30 MINUTES PLUS 2 HOURS 15 MINUTES PROVING
BAKE 🕐 35 MINUTES | OVEN 190°C (FAN)/210°C/425°F/GAS MARK 7

A soft, squidgy and delicious loaf, made superbly tender by the addition of cooked potato and sour cream. It may seem a faff getting everything together but this loaf tops my favourites list!

INGREDIENTS

110g (4oz) potato, boiled and cooled (approximately 1 medium potato)
375g (13oz) strong white bread flour
1 tsp salt
1½ tsp fast action yeast
150ml/120g (5fl oz/4oz) soured cream
90ml/90g (3¼fl oz/3¼oz) water, lukewarm
Oil for greasing
125g (4½oz) smoked bacon lardons
50g (1¾oz) mature cheddar cheese, grated
Oil for greasing

EQUIPMENT

Frying pan
Colander
Dish towel
Baking sheet

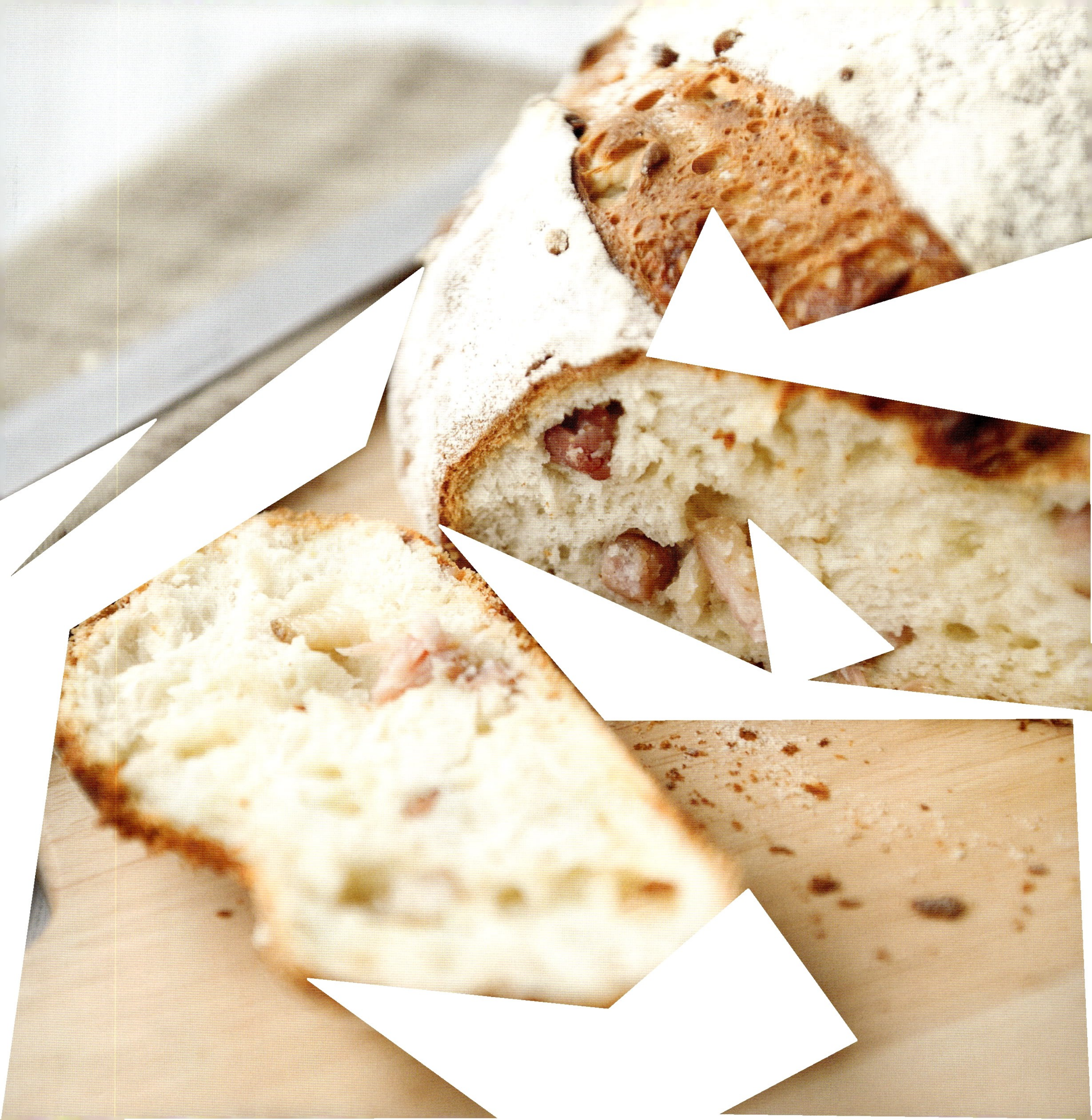

1 Grate the potato or mash roughly and combine in a large bowl with the flour, salt and yeast. Make a well in the centre and add the soured cream and water. This dough takes slightly longer to get going and rise than others because the dough temperature is lowered by the cold soured cream. If you can't wait, the water can be a little warmer than lukewarm – aim for hand hot. Mix together to form a rough dough.

2 Knead for 10 minutes until the dough turns smooth and elastic. There will still be lumps of potato in there so it isn't supposed to get completely smooth, don't worry! Transfer to a lightly oiled bowl, cover and allow to rise for 1½ hours or until doubled in size.

> **TIP**
> This is a fairly sticky dough to begin with – if that puts you off make the dough in the machine.

3 While the dough rises add the smoked bacon lardons to a frying pan and cook until lightly golden. Transfer to a bowl and allow to cool.

4 Turn the risen dough out onto the work surface and pat it with your hands to knock it back and spread it out a little. Scatter over the cooked bacon lardons and the grated cheese. Gather the dough together and knead gently for a couple of minutes to incorporate the cheese and bacon evenly. Place it back in the bowl to rest for 5 minutes – this will make the shaping easier.

5 Line a colander with a cotton dish towel and dust liberally with flour.

TIP The folding in technique after a first rise should successfully create a spine for a free form loaf which will enable the loaf to rise upwards rather than flowing outwards.

TIP
Special baskets can be bought for shaping loaves but they can be expensive – a colander or large sieve lined with a cotton dish towel and dusted with flour will do exactly the same job.

6 Take the dough out of the bowl and pat it out once again. Fold each outside edge in to the centre, repeating all the way round. Repeat again, folding the outside to the middle until the dough is tightened up into a rough ball. Pop the ball of dough into the lined colander with the seam upwards.

7 Fold the overhanging edges of the dish towel over the exposed dough and place in a warm position to rise until almost doubled in size, approximately 45 minutes. Preheat the oven to 190°C (fan)/210°C/425°F/Gas Mark 7.

8 Line a baking sheet with baking (parchment) paper or grease well. Unfold the dish towel and place the tray over the top of the colander. Invert the tray and colander together then remove the colander and dish towel. Dust the loaf with a little more flour and slash the top in a square pattern using a very sharp knife.

9 Bake in the preheated oven for 35 minutes. When it's baked through remove from the oven and transfer to a wire rack to cool completely. The crust will be firm as soon as it comes out of the oven but will soften on cooling to leave you with a tender loaf and crust.

Bacon & Cheese Potato Bread

CHORIZO & CHILLI POTATO BREAD

Here's a potato loaf with a kick! Gloriously tender bread hiding chunks of chorizo and a good sizzle of chilli.

MAKES 1 ROUND LOAF
PREP 30 MINUTES PLUS 2 HOURS 15 MINUTES PROVING
BAKE 35 MINUTES
OVEN 190°C (FAN)/210°C/425°F/GAS MARK 7

INGREDIENTS

110g (4oz) potato, boiled and cooled (approximately 1 medium potato)
375g (13oz) strong white bread flour
1 tsp salt
1½ tsp fast action yeast
150ml/120g (5fl oz/4oz) soured cream
90ml/90g (3¼fl oz/3¼oz) water, lukewarm
100g (3½oz) diced chorizo
1 red chilli, finely diced
Oil for greasing

EQUIPMENT

Baking sheet
Frying pan
Colander
Dish towel

1. Make the dough as for the Bacon & Cheese Potato Bread and set aside to rise.
2. Lightly fry the chorizo in a pan until golden. Transfer to a small bowl along with any oils released in the frying and allow to cool.
3. Once the dough has doubled in size gently knead in the chorizo and diced chilli until evenly combined, then proceed as for the Bacon & Cheese Potato Bread, shaping and proving in a cloth-lined colander, then turning onto a baking sheet. Slash the top and bake in the oven for 35 minutes. Transfer to a wire rack to cool.

TIP
If you prefer things a little less spicy deseed the chilli before finely dicing.

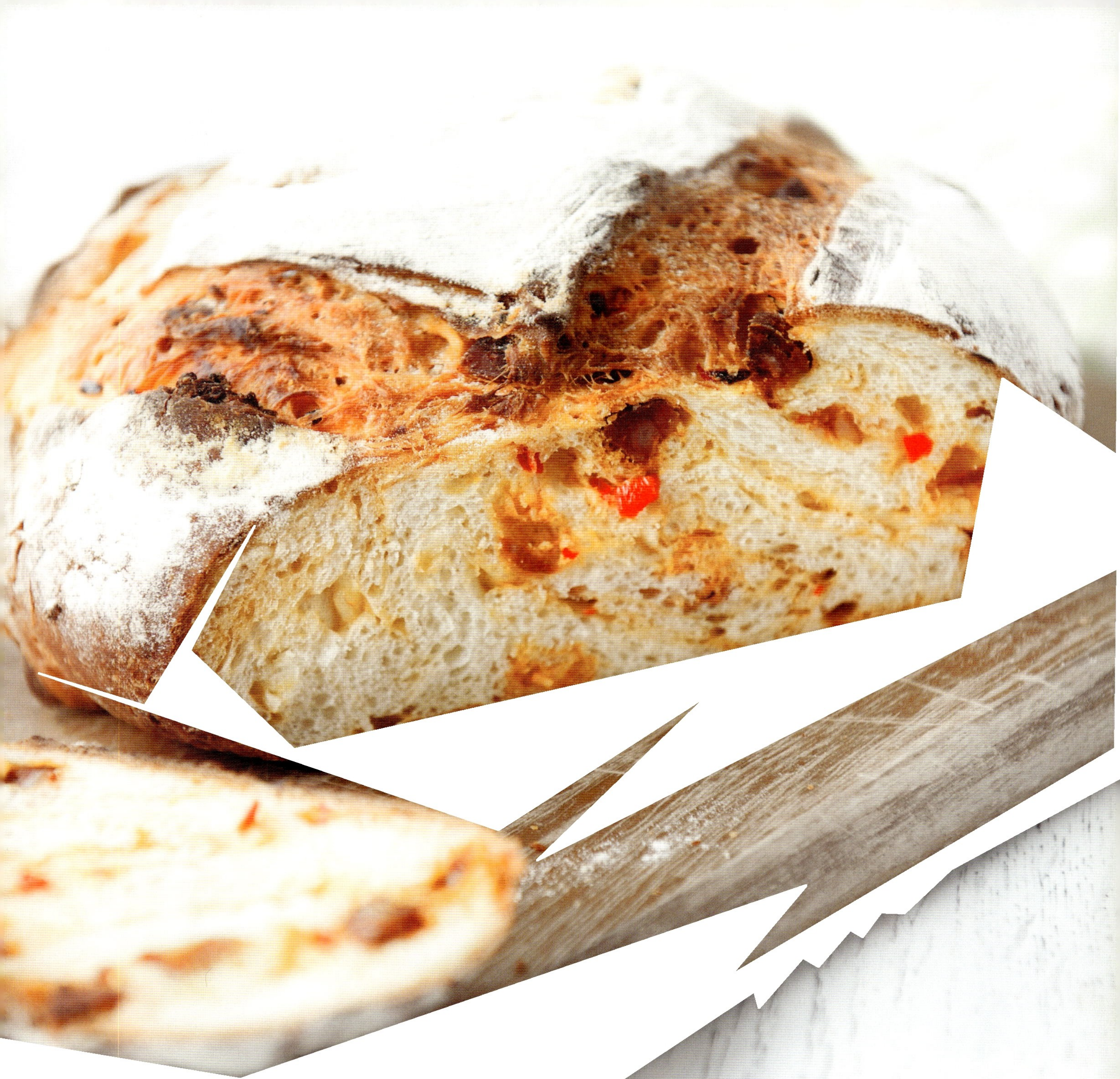

SPICED CHOCOLATE ORANGE FINGERS

MAKES 8 FINGER ROLLS
PREP ⏲ 30 MINUTES PLUS 1½ HOURS PROVING
BAKE ⏲ 12 MINUTES | OVEN 190°C (FAN)/210°C/425°F/GAS MARK 7

Gently spiced orange-scented rolls topped with chocolate glaze – who could resist one of these?

INGREDIENTS
Rolls

250g (9oz) strong white bread flour

25g (1oz) caster (superfine) sugar

½ tsp salt

1½ tsp fast action yeast

Zest of 1 orange

1 tsp ground cinnamon

1 tsp ground cloves

Pinch of cayenne pepper

30g (1oz) softened butter

1 egg, large

100ml/103g (3½fl oz/3¾oz) milk, lukewarm

Oil for greasing

35g (1¼oz) grated dark (bittersweet) chocolate

Glaze

120g (4oz) icing (confectioners') sugar, sifted

30g (1oz) cocoa powder

1 tbsp glucose

2–3 tbsp water

EQUIPMENT

Zester

Grater

Baking sheet

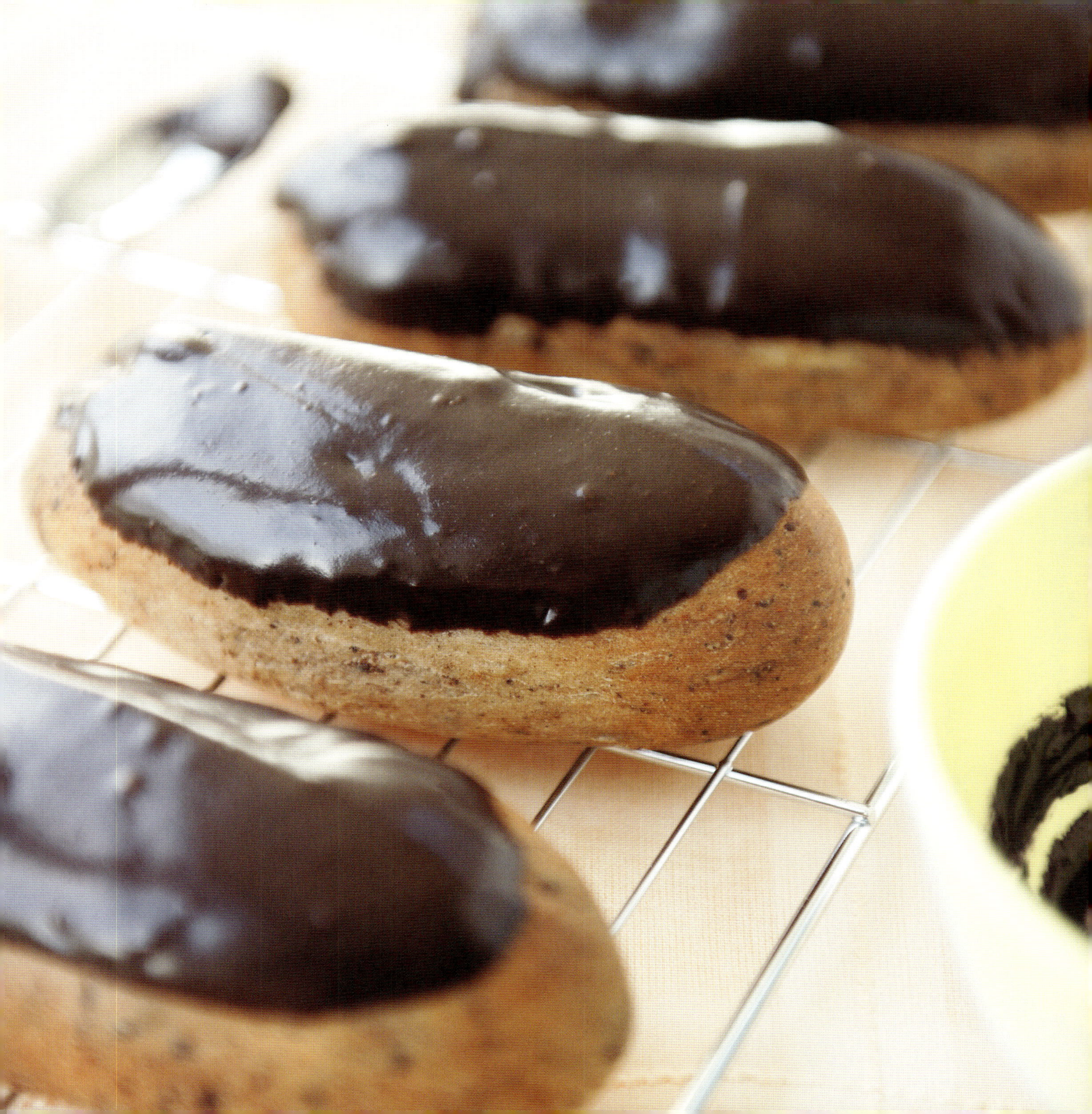

1 In a large bowl combine the strong white bread flour, caster (superfine) sugar, salt, yeast, orange zest and spices. Make a well in the centre and add the softened butter, egg and milk.

2 Work the wet and dry ingredients together to form a rough dough, then knead for 10 minutes until smooth and elastic. Transfer to a lightly oiled bowl, cover with cling film (plastic wrap) and allow to rise for 1 hour or until doubled in size.

3 Tip the dough out onto the work surface and knead very lightly for 1 minute. Flatten the dough out into a rectangle shape and scatter over the grated chocolate.

4 Fold the dough over, enclosing the chocolate. Knead again until the grated chocolate is dispersed evenly.

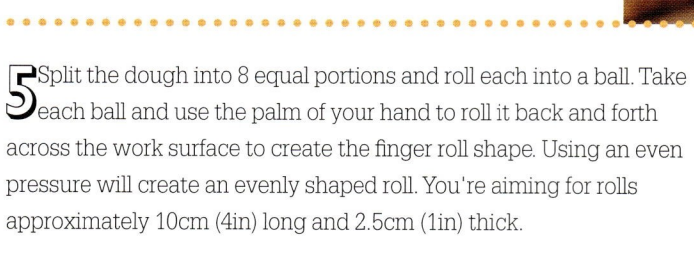

5 Split the dough into 8 equal portions and roll each into a ball. Take each ball and use the palm of your hand to roll it back and forth across the work surface to create the finger roll shape. Using an even pressure will create an evenly shaped roll. You're aiming for rolls approximately 10cm (4in) long and 2.5cm (1in) thick.

6 Transfer the shaped rolls to a lined or well greased baking sheet, spaced apart to allow for spreading. Cover with cling film (plastic wrap) and allow to rise for 30 minutes or until nearly doubled in size. Preheat the oven to 200°C (fan)/220°C/425°F/Gas Mark 7.

7 Bake in the preheated oven for 12 minutes. When baked transfer to a wire rack and allow to cool completely.

8 To make the glaze, sift together the icing sugar and cocoa powder into a wide, shallow bowl, then add the liquid glucose. Add the water 1 tablespoon at a time and mix well to form a glossy icing – the consistency should be fairly thick but not so thick that you can't dip the tops of the rolls in.

TIP
The glucose in the icing can easily be found in the baking aisle of most supermarkets. The glaze can be made without it using a little extra water in its place if you prefer – it just won't be as glossy.

9 Dip the top of each roll into the glaze in a pendulum type motion, moving the roll steadily through and out of the glaze. As you move the roll out of the glaze wipe any excess from the end on the edge of your bowl or with a finger. Set on a wire rack, glaze-side up, and allow the glaze to set.

Spiced Chocolate Orange Fingers

ICED LEMON FINGERS

The simple flavour of a lemon finger will be a hit with whoever you decide to share these with.

MAKES 8 FINGER ROLLS
PREP 25 MINUTES PLUS 1½ HOURS PROVING
BAKE 12 MINUTES
OVEN 190°C (FAN)/210°C/425°F/GAS MARK 7

TIP
If there is not enough lemon juice to get to the right consistency for the glaze use a little water.

INGREDIENTS
Rolls

250g (9oz) strong white bread flour
25g (1oz) caster (superfine) sugar
½ tsp salt
1½ tsp fast action yeast
100ml/103g (3½fl oz/3¾oz) milk, lukewarm
30g (1oz) softened butter
1 egg, large
Zest of 1 lemon

Glaze

150g (5½oz) icing (confectioners') sugar
1 tbsp glucose
2-3 tbsp lemon juice

EQUIPMENT
Zester
Grater
Baking sheet

1. Make the dough for the rolls as for the Spiced Chocolate Orange Fingers, simply omitting the spices and replacing the orange zest with lemon zest. There's nothing to work in when lightly kneading the dough before shaping into finger rolls.

2. Once baked, glaze in the same way, making up the glaze with freshly squeezed lemon juice instead of water and omitting the cocoa powder.

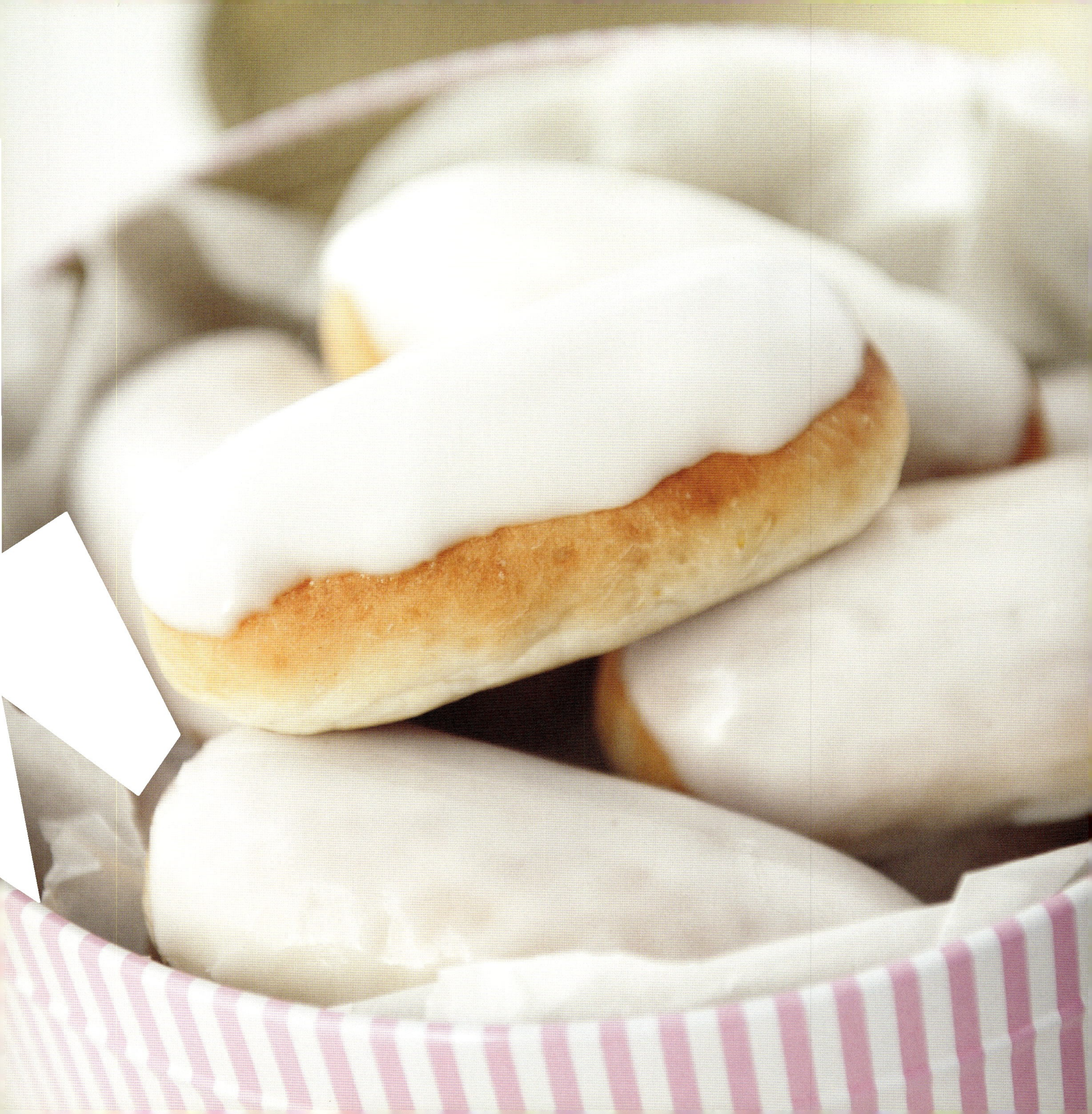

PERFECT PRE-FERMENT

Bread made with a pre-ferment may seem like a bit of a faff but trust me – it isn't. Simply mix up the pre-ferment last thing at night and then leave it in a cool kitchen or in the fridge until the morning. Because the pre-ferment is allowed to develop overnight the flavours become intensified, producing a far superior loaf in the taste department.

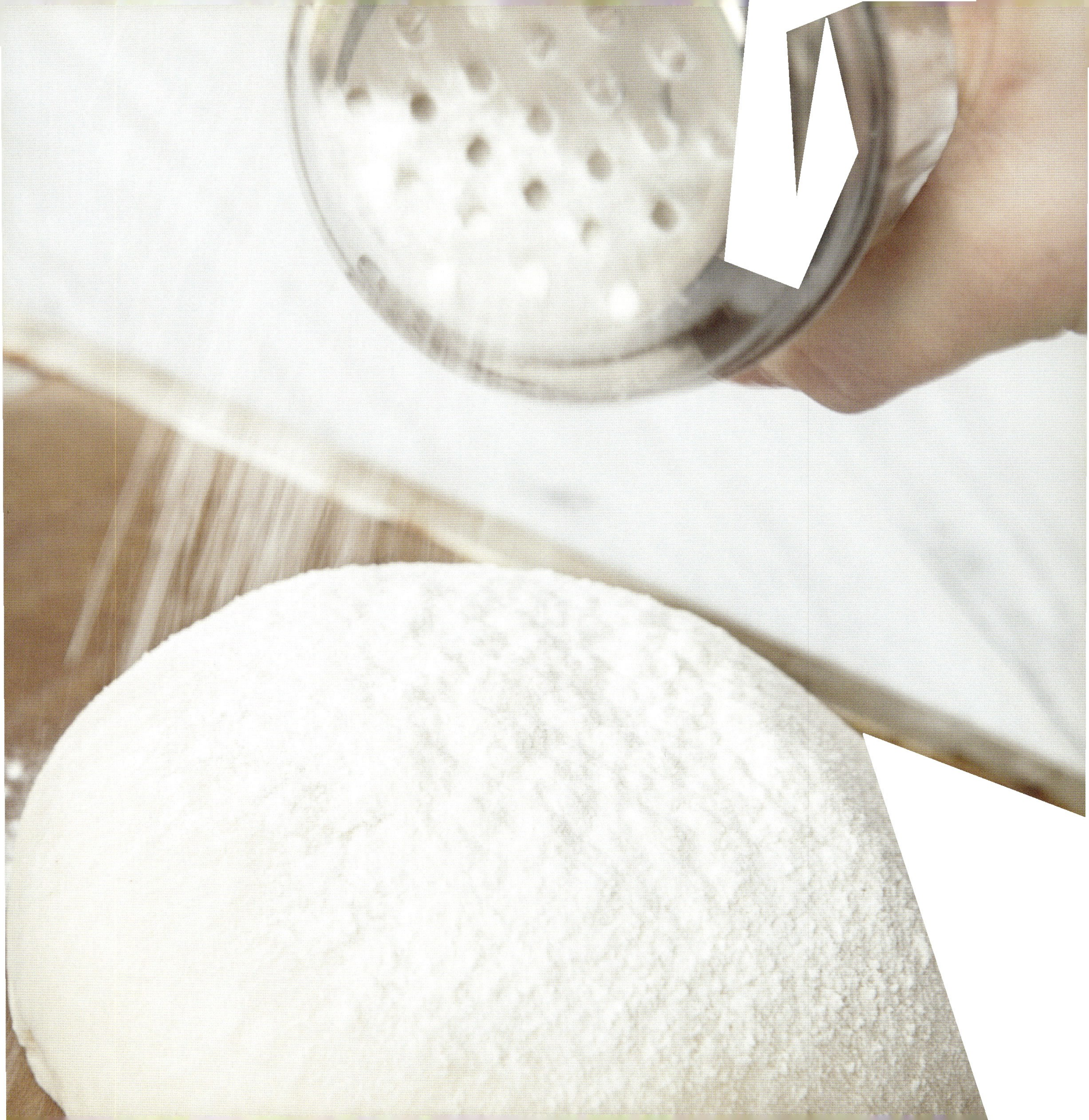

CRUSTY COBB

MAKES ONE LARGE ROUND LOAF
PREP 40 MINUTES PLUS OVERNIGHT DEVELOPMENT OF PRE-FERMENT AND 1½ HOURS PROVING
BAKE 35 MINUTES | OVEN 200°C (FAN)/220°C/425°F/GAS MARK 7

Who can resist a Crusty Cobb? It has a crust so crispy you can hear it crackle as it cools. The pre-ferment adds tons of flavour and the steam works its magic on the loaf as it begins to bake.

INGREDIENTS

Pre-Ferment
250g (9oz) strong white bread flour
2 tsp instant dried yeast
290ml/290g (10¼fl oz/10¼oz) water

Dough
250g (9oz) strong white flour (white bread flour)
1 tsp salt
1 tsp caster (superfine) sugar
55g (2oz) butter, melted and cooled

EQUIPMENT

Sharp knife
Large baking sheet
Roasting pan

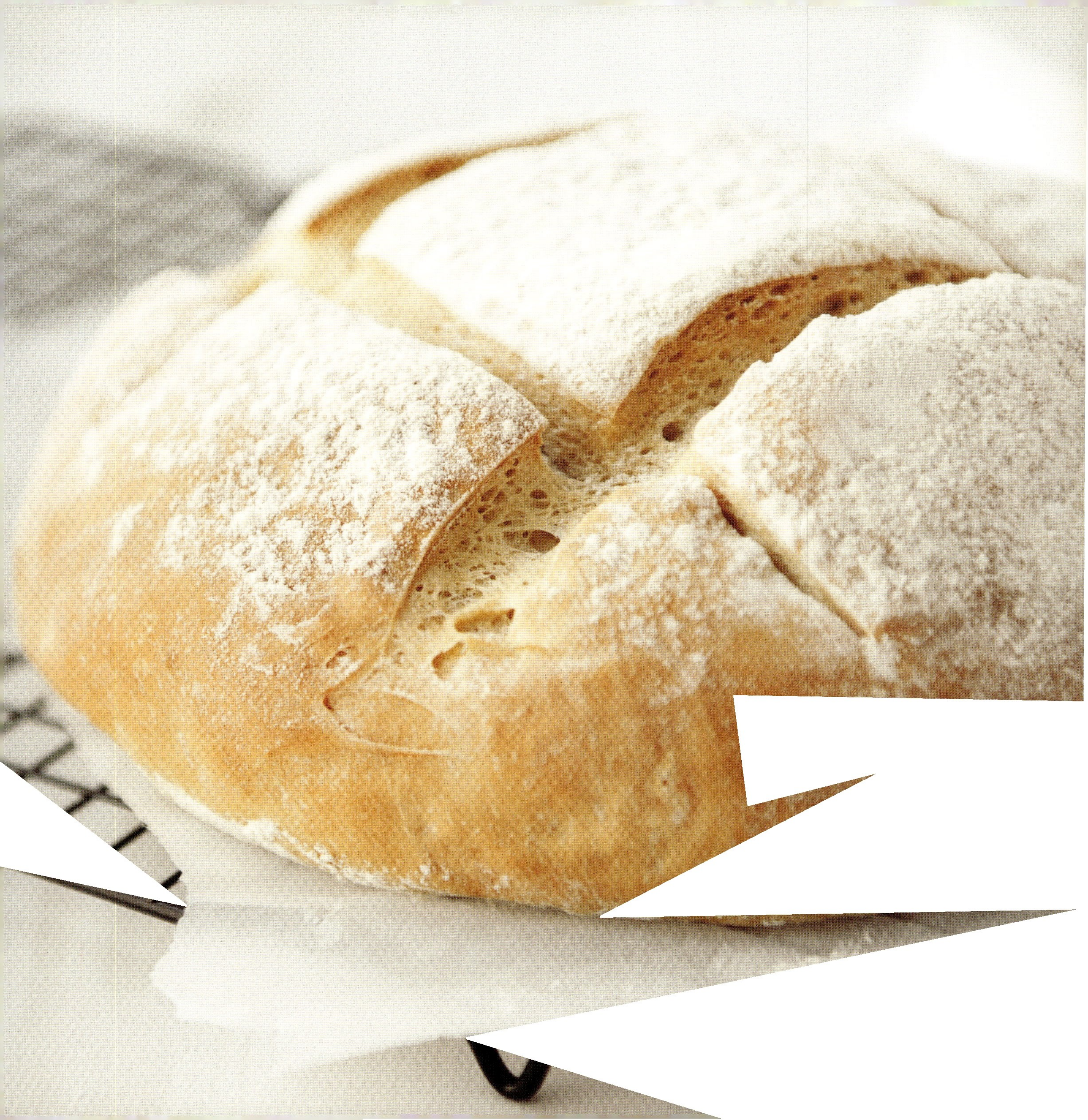

1 Start off by making the pre-ferment. Mix together the strong white bread flour, yeast and water (cold water is fine) in a bowl. It doesn't have to be super smooth, some lumps of flour are fine. Just make sure the bowl is big enough to allow for an increase in volume. Cover with cling film (plastic wrap) and allow it to develop either in a cool room or in the fridge for at least 4 hours; ideally overnight.

2 Once developed the pre-ferment should be bubbly and will have increased in volume.

TIP
Plastic dough scrapers are a great investment if you're making bread often, but a silicone spatula will work in much the same way for scraping dough from bowls.

3 Add the dough ingredients (strong white bread flour, salt, sugar and cooled melted butter) to the pre-ferment mixture. Mix to a rough dough and then knead on the work surface for 10 minutes until smooth.

4 Transfer the dough to a lightly oiled bowl, cover with cling film or a clean dish towel and allow to rise for 1 hour or until doubled in size. Once risen, tip the dough out onto the work surface and knead lightly for two minutes to work out any large air bubbles.

5 Flatten the dough into a rough circle. Taking the outside edge of the dough fold it in to the middle and work in this way all around the outside edge until you get back to where you started and can fold in no more!

6 Flip the dough over so that the seam is underneath. Gently cup your hands around the ball of dough and start to tighten the dough again, moving your hands down and underneath it, repeating until the dough feels tight like a coiled spring. Repeat the tightening action, gently encouraging the dough into a round shape, all the time keeping the seam underneath. The shaping is important in getting a free-form loaf to rise upwards and keep its shape rather than flowing outwards.

Crusty Cobb **65**

7 Set the loaf onto a baking sheet lined with baking (parchment) paper. Cover with a clean dish towel and position in a draught-free spot to prove for 30 minutes or until nearly doubled in size. Place a sturdy metal roasting tin in the bottom of the oven and position your baking shelf in the centre of the oven. Preheat the oven to 200°C (fan)/220°C/425°F/Gas Mark 7.

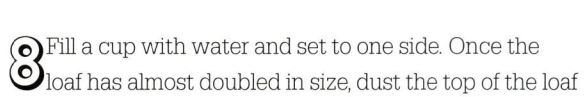

8 Fill a cup with water and set to one side. Once the loaf has almost doubled in size, dust the top of the loaf with a little flour.

TIP
If you're not happy with the shape of the loaf when it has risen and it's looking shallow and flat, you can reshape it at this stage, working hard to form a good spine, and prove it again.

TIP

Make sure you spend time shaping a free-form loaf so that it rises upwards instead of outwards across the baking sheet. Folding in and tightening the dough forms a 'spine' for the loaf that gives it vital structure.

9 Now it's time to bake. Slash the top of the loaf with a sharp knife – 2 cuts lengthways and 2 widthways. Slashing the tops of loaves takes confidence, so no dithering! Slash quickly and confidently with a super sharp knife so that the dough doesn't collapse underneath the blade.

10 Place the loaf in the oven, then pour the cup of water into the roasting tin at the base and quickly close the door. The water creates a flurry of steam that will help to create an extra crispy crust. Bake for 35 minutes and then remove from the oven and transfer to a wire rack to cool.

Crusty Cobb

TIGER BREAD

Create a stunning Tiger Loaf with a crispy crunchy tiger topping. The sesame oil adds a hint of nuttiness but can be substituted for regular vegetable or sunflower oil if you prefer.

MAKES ONE LARGE OVAL LOAF
PREP 🕐 45 MINUTES PLUS OVERNIGHT DEVELOPMENT OF PRE-FERMENT AND 1½ HOURS PROVING
BAKE 🕐 35 MINUTES
OVEN 200ºC (FAN)/220°C/425°F/GAS MARK 7

INGREDIENTS
Pre-Ferment
250g (9oz) strong white bread flour
2 tsp instant dried yeast
290ml/290g (10¼fl oz/10¼oz) water

Dough
250g (9oz) strong white bread flour
1 tsp salt
1 tsp caster (superfine) sugar
55g (2oz) butter, melted and cooled

Tiger Paste
¼ tsp instant dried yeast
¼ tsp caster (superfine) sugar
13g (½oz) rice flour
1 tsp sesame oil
1 tbsp warm water

EQUIPMENT
Palette knife
Large baking sheet
Roasting pan

1. Make the pre-ferment and the dough as for the Crusty Cobb recipe.
2. When it comes to shaping the loaf, instead of working it into a round aim for a longer, slightly tapered loaf shape and set it onto a well greased or lined baking sheet.
3. Mix together the dry ingredients for the tiger paste and then add in the oil and water. Mix to a firm paste.
4. Using a palette knife spread the paste thinly over the top and sides of the loaf. It is a scant amount and it does need to be thin to create the distinctive crackle top.
5. Allow the loaf to rise in a warm spot, uncovered, for 30 minutes or until nearly doubled in size. The rise of the dough will cause the paste to crack and create the distinctive 'tiger' pattern. Bake in the preheated oven for 35 minutes, adding the cup of water to the preheated roasting pan in the base of the oven to create steam. Allow to cool on a wire rack.

TIP
If your tiger paste is too dry to spread, add a drop of water a tiny, tiny bit at a time to loosen it slightly. It does need to be on the thick side so that it will split as the dough proves for the final time.

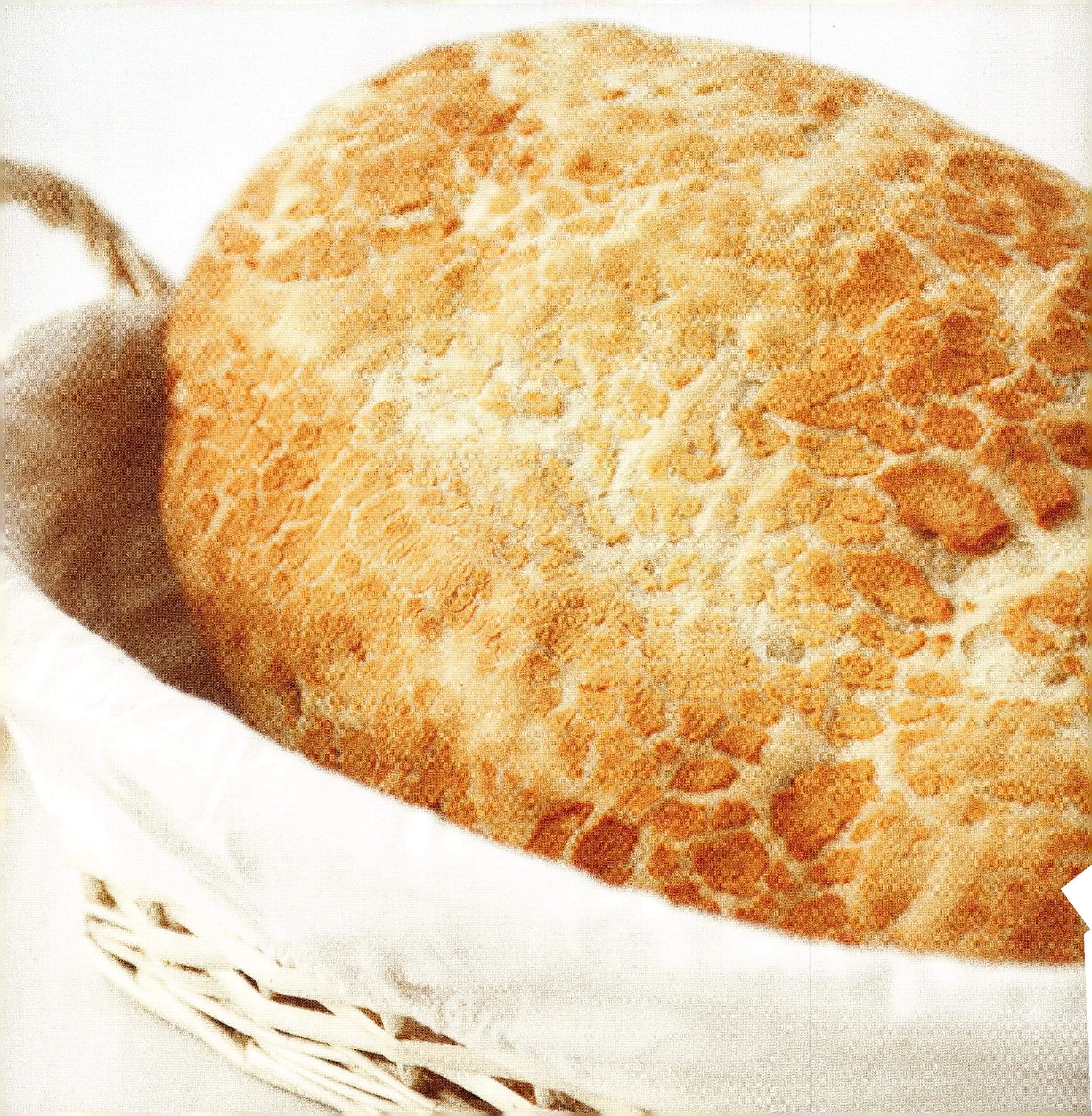

SEEDED MULTIGRAIN LOAF

MAKES 1 LARGE TIN (PAN) LOAF
**PREP 🕐 40 MINUTES PLUS OVERNIGHT DEVELOPMENT
OF THE PRE-FERMENT AND 3 HOURS PROVING**
BAKE 🕐 35 MINUTES | OVEN 190°C (FAN)/210°C/425°F/GAS MARK 7

A dark, mixed-grain loaf using a combination of white, wholemeal (whole wheat) and rye flours. If you like your bread flavoursome and packed with crunchy seeds then this is the loaf for you.

INGREDIENTS
Pre-Ferment
100g (2½oz) strong white bread flour
65g (2¼oz) wholemeal (whole wheat) bread flour
65g (2¼oz) rye flour
2½ tsp fast action yeast
2 tbsp treacle (molasses)
310ml/320g (11fl oz/11½oz) milk, cold

Dough
125g (4½oz) strong white bread flour
60g (2¼oz) wholemeal bread flour
60g (2¼oz) rye flour
1 tsp salt
Oil for greasing

Seed Mix
1 tbsp golden linseeds (flaxseeds)
1 tbsp poppy seeds
1 tbsp sesame seeds
1 tbsp sunflower seeds
1 tbsp plus 1 tsp pumpkin seeds

EQUIPMENT
900g (2lb) Loaf tin (pan)

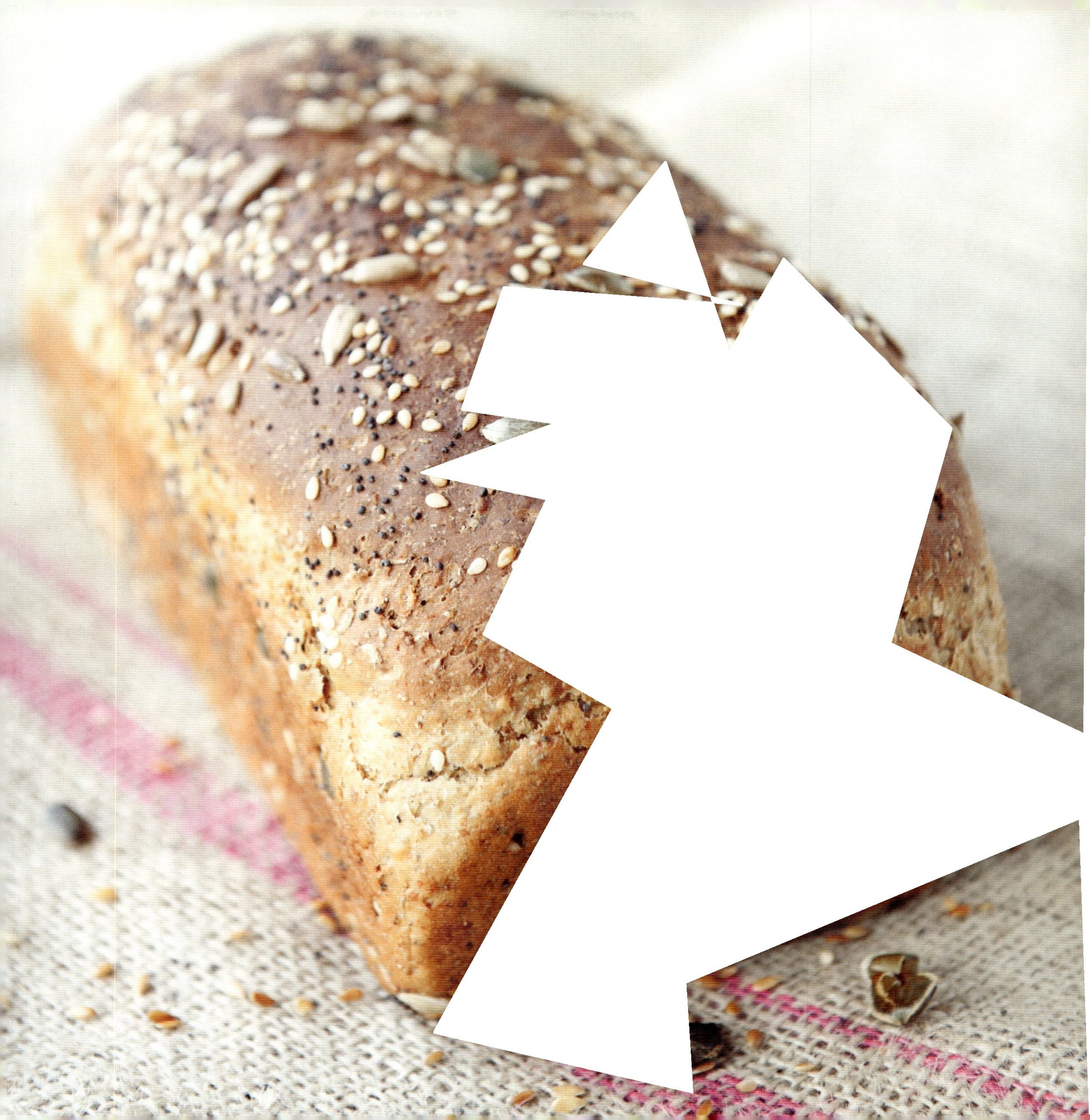

1. Start off by making the pre-ferment. Mix together the flours, yeast, treacle (molasses) and milk in a bowl. Work the mixture together with a fork until there are no large pockets of flour. It will be a little lumpy at this stage. Cover with cling film (plastic wrap) and allow to develop either in a cool kitchen or in the fridge for a minimum of 4 hours; ideally overnight.

2. Once developed the pre-ferment should be bubbly and will have increased in volume.

3. Add the dough ingredients to the developed pre-ferment and mix to a rough dough. Knead on the work surface for 10 minutes until smooth. Transfer the dough to a lightly oiled bowl, cover with cling film (plastic wrap) or a clean dish towel and allow to rise for 2 hours or until doubled in size.

TIP
If your pre-ferment has been in the fridge overnight the temperature of the dough will be cool and as a result it will take longer to rise. Don't rush it: wait until the dough is ready before moving on to the next stage. Patience is important!

4 Mix the seeds together in a small bowl. Take a tablespoon of the seed mix and set to one side.

5 Once risen, tip the dough out onto the work surface and knead lightly for two minutes to work out any large air bubbles. Flatten the dough into a rough circle. Scatter over the bowl of seed mix. Fold the dough in to the centre to enclose the seeds and knead for a couple of minutes until the seeds are evenly distributed.

6 Flatten the dough out into a rough rectangle and fold the outside edges in to the centre, repeating all the way around. Repeat this action again, tightening up the dough and forming the spine for the loaf. Once the dough can't be folded in any more flip it over so that the seam sits underneath. Gently roll the dough into a loaf shape. Take the 1 tbsp of seed mix reserved earlier and scatter it over the work surface. Roll the loaf through the seeds to coat the top and sides.

7 Place the loaf in a well-greased loaf tin (pan), cover and set to one side to rise until it just curves above the top of the tin (pan) (about an hour). Preheat the oven to 190°C (fan)/210°C/425°F/Gas Mark 7.

8 Bake in the preheated oven for 35 minutes. Turn out right away and transfer to a wire rack to cool completely.

Seeded Multigrain Loaf

MAPLE & PECAN LOAF

A slightly lighter version of the Seeded Multigrain Loaf without the seeds but still packed with the nutty taste of wholemeal and rye flours and a good crunch from the pecans.

MAKES 1 LARGE TIN (PAN) LOAF
PREP 40 MINUTES PLUS OVERNIGHT DEVELOPMENT OF THE PRE-FERMENT AND 3 HOURS PROVING
BAKE 35 MINUTES
OVEN 190°C (FAN)/210°C/425°F/GAS MARK 7

TIP
Replace the pecans with your favourite nuts – try walnuts or even pine nuts.

INGREDIENTS
Pre-Ferment

100g (2½oz) strong white bread flour
65g (2¼oz) wholemeal (whole wheat) bread flour
65g (2¼oz) rye flour
2½ tsp fast action yeast
2 tbsp maple syrup
310ml/320g (11fl oz/11½oz) milk, cold

Dough

125g (4½oz) strong white bread flour
60g (2¼oz) wholemeal bread flour
60g (2¼oz) rye flour
1 tsp salt
Oil for greasing
60g (2¼oz) pecans, roughly chopped

EQUIPMENT
900g (2lb) Loaf tin (pan)

1. Make the pre-ferment and the dough in the same way as the Seeded Multigrain Loaf, substituting the treacle (molasses) for maple syrup.

2. Work the roughly chopped pecans into the dough in place of the seed mix. Generously flour the top of the risen loaf, slash the top with a sharp knife and bake in the preheated oven for 35 minutes. Allow to cool on a wire rack.

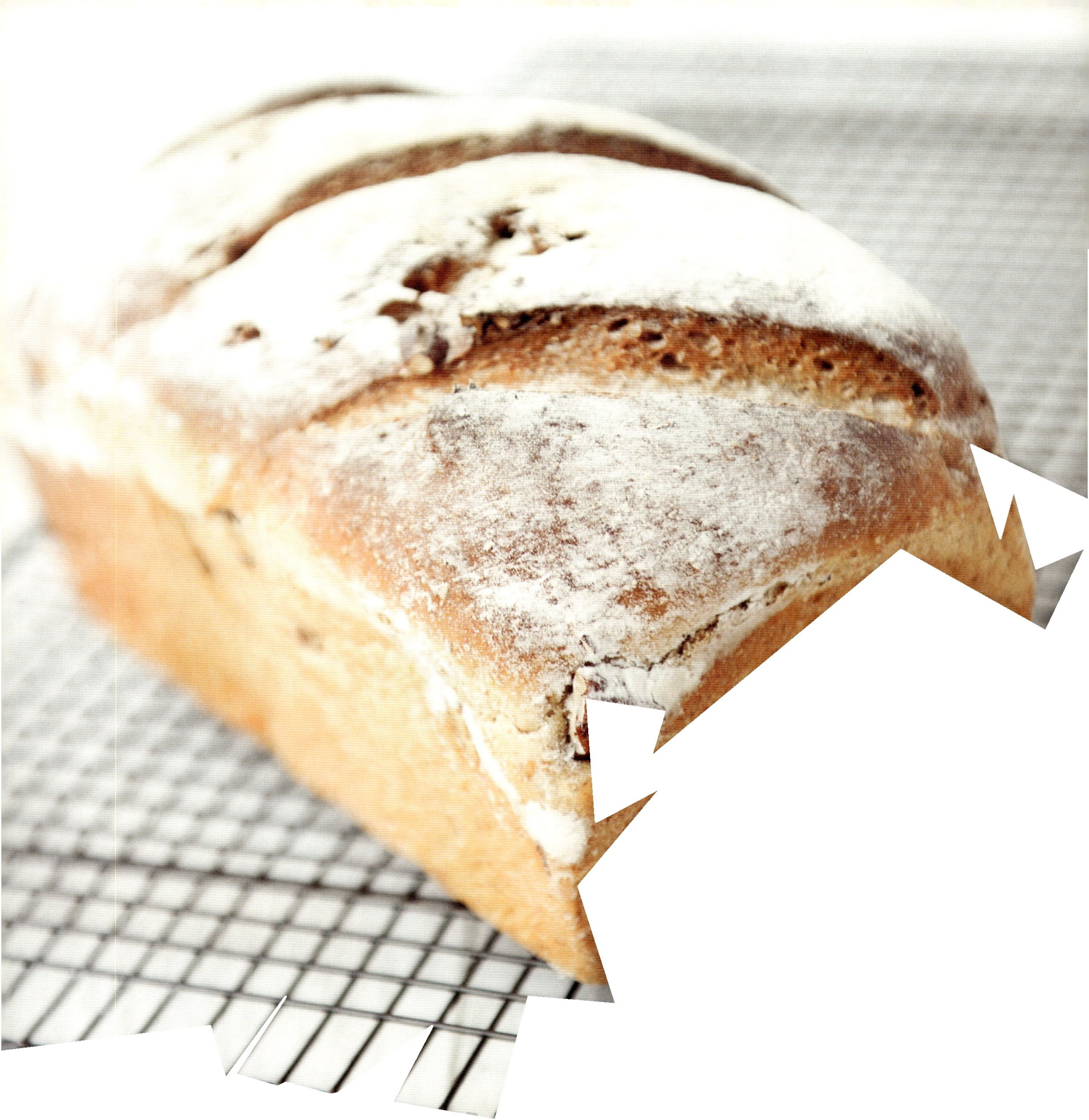

DANISH APPLE PLAIT

MAKES 1 PLAIT
PREP ⏲ 1 HOUR PLUS 4 HOURS OR OVERNIGHT DEVELOPMENT
OF THE PRE-FERMENT AND 2 HOURS PROVING
BAKE ⏲ 25 MINUTES | OVEN 180°C (FAN)/200°C/400°F/GAS MARK 6

This loaf is just as good eaten cold as it is warm from the oven with a generous helping of cream or custard.

INGREDIENTS
Pre-Ferment
100g (3½oz) strong white bread flour
2 tsp fast action yeast
125ml/125g (4½fl oz/4½oz) apple juice, cold

Dough
200g (7oz) strong white bread flour
½ tsp salt
30g (1oz) caster (superfine) sugar
1 large egg
Oil for greasing

Filling
100g (3½oz) marzipan
200g (7oz) diced cooking apple, peeled and cored (1 medium cooking apple, approximately 275g (9¾oz) unpeeled weight)
1 tsp cinnamon
30g (1oz) light muscovado sugar
1 tbsp icing (confectioners') sugar

Glaze
1 egg, beaten

EQUIPMENT
Baking sheet
Pastry brush

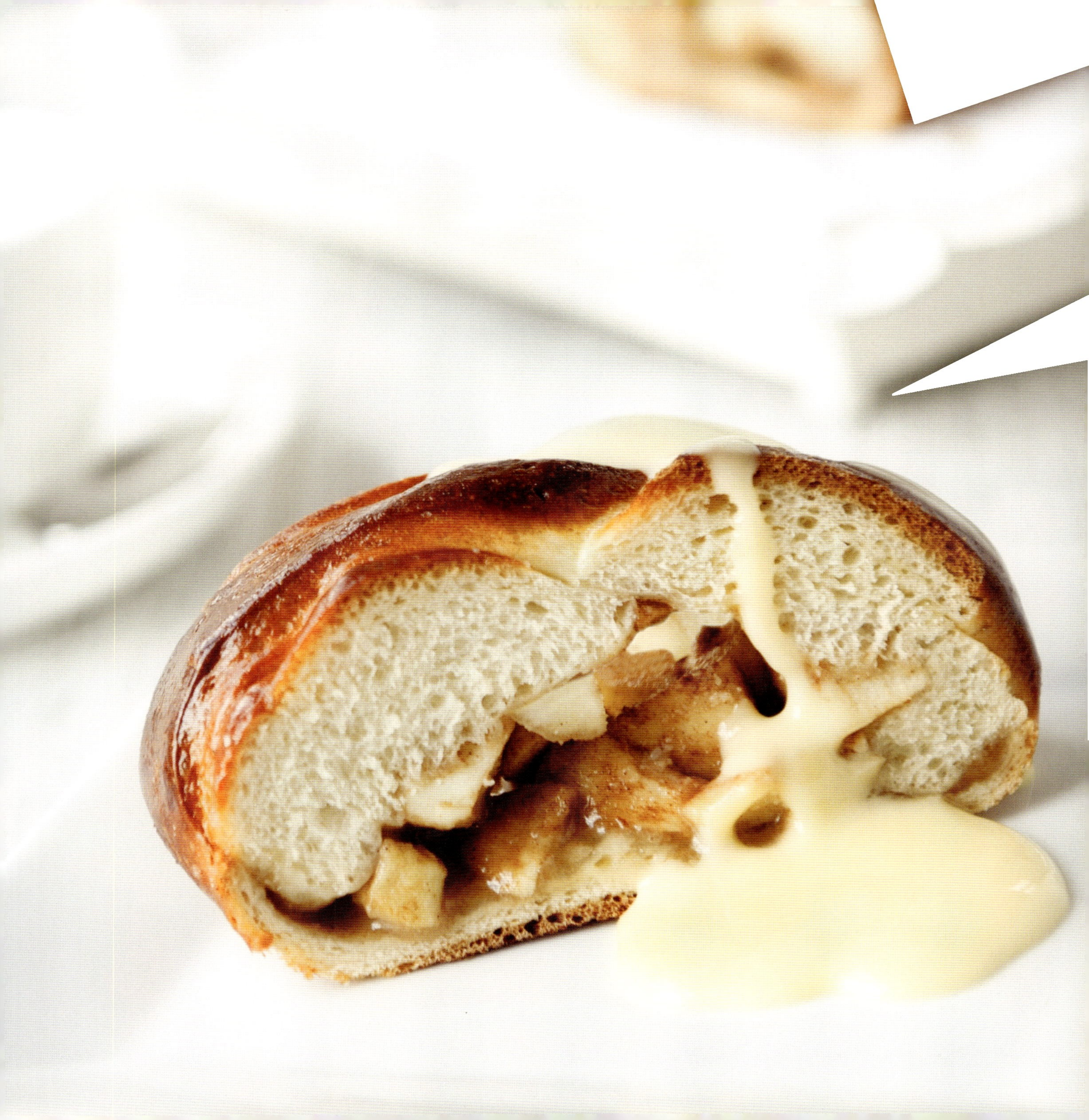

1 Mix together the ingredients for the pre-ferment in a bowl. Cover it with cling film (plastic wrap) and allow to develop either in a cool kitchen or in the fridge for at least 4 hours; preferably overnight. Once developed, the pre-ferment should be bubbly and will have increased in volume.

2 Add the dough ingredients to the developed pre-ferment. Mix to a rough dough and then knead on the work surface for 10 minutes until smooth. Transfer the dough to a lightly oiled bowl, cover with cling film (plastic wrap) or a clean dish towel and allow to rise for 1½ hours or until doubled in size.

3 Place the marzipan in the freezer – this makes it easy to grate later. Peel, core and dice the cooking apple and toss together with the cinnamon and muscovado sugar.

4 Put 1 tbsp icing (confectioners') sugar in a bowl. Remove the marzipan from the freezer and grate over the sugar, tossing the grated pieces regularly in it to prevent them from clumping together. Set both the apple mixture and the grated marzipan to one side.

5 Turn out the dough onto the work surface. It will still feel a little oily from the oil in the bowl so you won't need any extra flour or oil on the surface to prevent it from sticking. Gently roll it out to a 30 x 30cm (12 x 12in) square. Gently press a finger at the bottom edge of the dough to mark the square into thirds.

6 Scatter the grated marzipan over the central third of the dough, leaving the top and bottom 6cm (2½in) clean. Spoon the apple mixture on top of the marzipan. Make vertical cuts at the top and bottom so that the central clean sections form flaps that you will fold in later. Now make diagonal cuts at a 45-degree angle from the top corner of the dough to the filling on each side. They should be about 2.5cm 1in) apart. Cut away the two triangles at the very top and bottom of each side.

7 Fold the flaps at the top and base down over the filling. Then take the top strip of dough from the left. Fold it diagonally over the filling, fold in the top strip from the right and overlap. Repeat the plaiting all the way down, one from the left, one from the right.

TIP This plait can easily be made in advance and then reheated in the oven for serving warm.

8 Carry on plaiting at the bottom so that the strips overhang the end of the loaf. Once fully plaited, tuck these underneath the loaf to seal in the filling. Carefully transfer the plait to a lined baking sheet: place the tray next to the plait and confidently scoop it up with both your hands supporting it – a fish slice may be useful here.

9 Cover the plait with a clean dish towel and place in a warm spot to rise until puffy and the dough almost doubled in size (30 minutes). Preheat the oven to 180°C (fan)/200°C/400°F/Gas Mark 6. When the plait is risen brush all over with beaten egg and bake in the preheated oven for 25 minutes until golden. Transfer to a wire rack to cool or serve immediately with custard!

Danish Apple Plait

PICNIC PLAIT

Instead of making sandwiches for a picnic why not try this picnic plait? The fillings are sealed inside so all you have to do is slice and serve – you won't believe how fast it disappears.

MAKES 1 PLAIT
PREP ⏲ 1 HOUR PLUS 4 HOURS OR OVERNIGHT DEVELOPMENT OF THE PRE-FERMENT AND 2 HOURS PROVING
BAKE ⏲ 25 MINUTES
OVEN 180°C (FAN)/200°C/400°F/GAS MARK 6

1. Make the pre-ferment using the same method as the Danish Apple Plait, but using water instead of apple juice.
2. When it comes to making the dough follow the Danish Apple Plait method but decrease the sugar to just 1 tsp, increase the salt to 1 tsp and add 1 tsp mustard powder.
3. To fill the plait, use half of the ham to fill the centre section with an even layer, followed by the quartered cherry tomatoes, diced mozzarella and basil leaves. Top with a second layer of ham. Plait the loaf, following the method in the Danish Apple Plait.
4. Transfer to a baking sheet and allow to rise until the dough is puffy and almost doubled in size. Brush with beaten egg and bake in the preheated oven for 25 minutes. Transfer to a wire rack and allow to cool completely.

INGREDIENTS

Pre-Ferment

100g (3½oz) strong white bread flour
2 tsp fast action yeast
125ml/125g (4½fl oz/4½oz) water, cold

Dough

200g (7oz) strong white bread flour
1 tsp salt
1 tsp mustard powder
1 tsp caster (superfine) sugar
1 large egg

Filling

125g (4½oz) (4–5 slices) of thick-cut roast ham
75g (2¾oz) cherry tomatoes, quartered
75g (2¾oz) mozzarella cheese, diced
Small handful of basil leaves

Glaze

1 egg, beaten

EQUIPMENT

Baking sheet
Pastry brush

TIP You can make up your own filling for this Picnic Plait to suit your own taste, but try to balance wet ingredients with dry ones e.g. tomato and ham. If you use a lot of wet fillings then the dough is likely to absorb the moisture and become soggy.

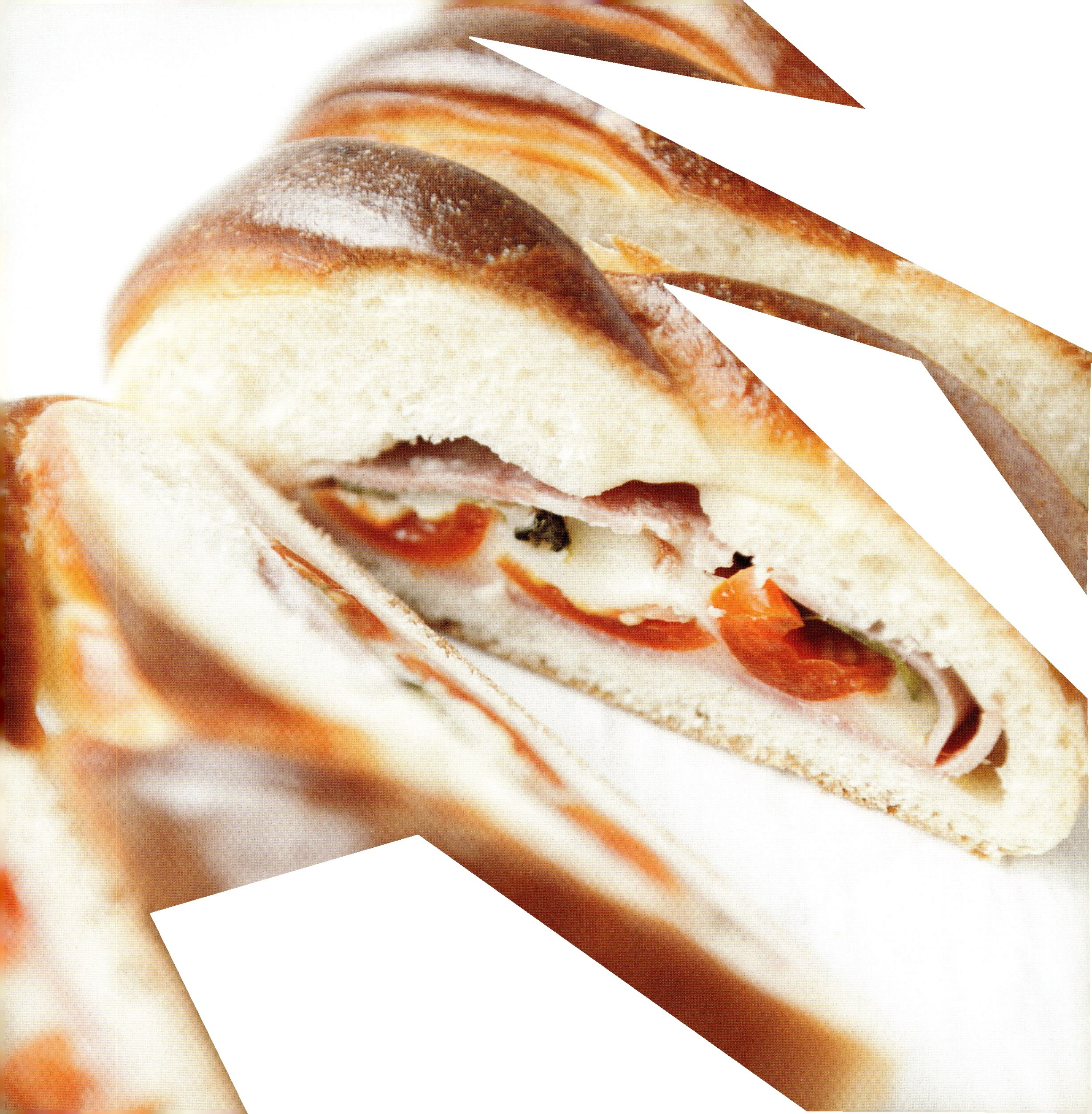

CIABATTA WITH OLIVE OIL

MAKES 3 SMALL LOAVES
PREP 🕐 **30 MINS PLUS 4 HOURS OR OVERNIGHT DEVELOPMENT OF THE PRE-FERMENT AND 3 HOURS 15 MINUTES PROVING**
BAKE 🕐 **38 MINUTES | OVEN 210°C (FAN)/230°C/450°F/GAS MARK 8 THEN 190°C (FAN)/210°C/425°F/GAS MARK 7**

This is a super-hydrated dough, almost bordering on a liquid state, and it takes gentle handling to keep in the large air bubbles characteristic of a classic Ciabatta. Follow the steps carefully and you'll have cracking Ciabatta loaves.

INGREDIENTS

Pre-Ferment

150g (5½oz) strong white bread flour
180ml/180g (6¼fl oz/6¼oz) water, cold
¼ tsp fast action yeast

Dough

325g (11½oz) strong white bread flour
175ml/175g (6fl oz/6oz) water
1½ tsp salt
1 tsp yeast
2 tbsp olive oil

EQUIPMENT

Baking (parchment) paper
Baking sheet

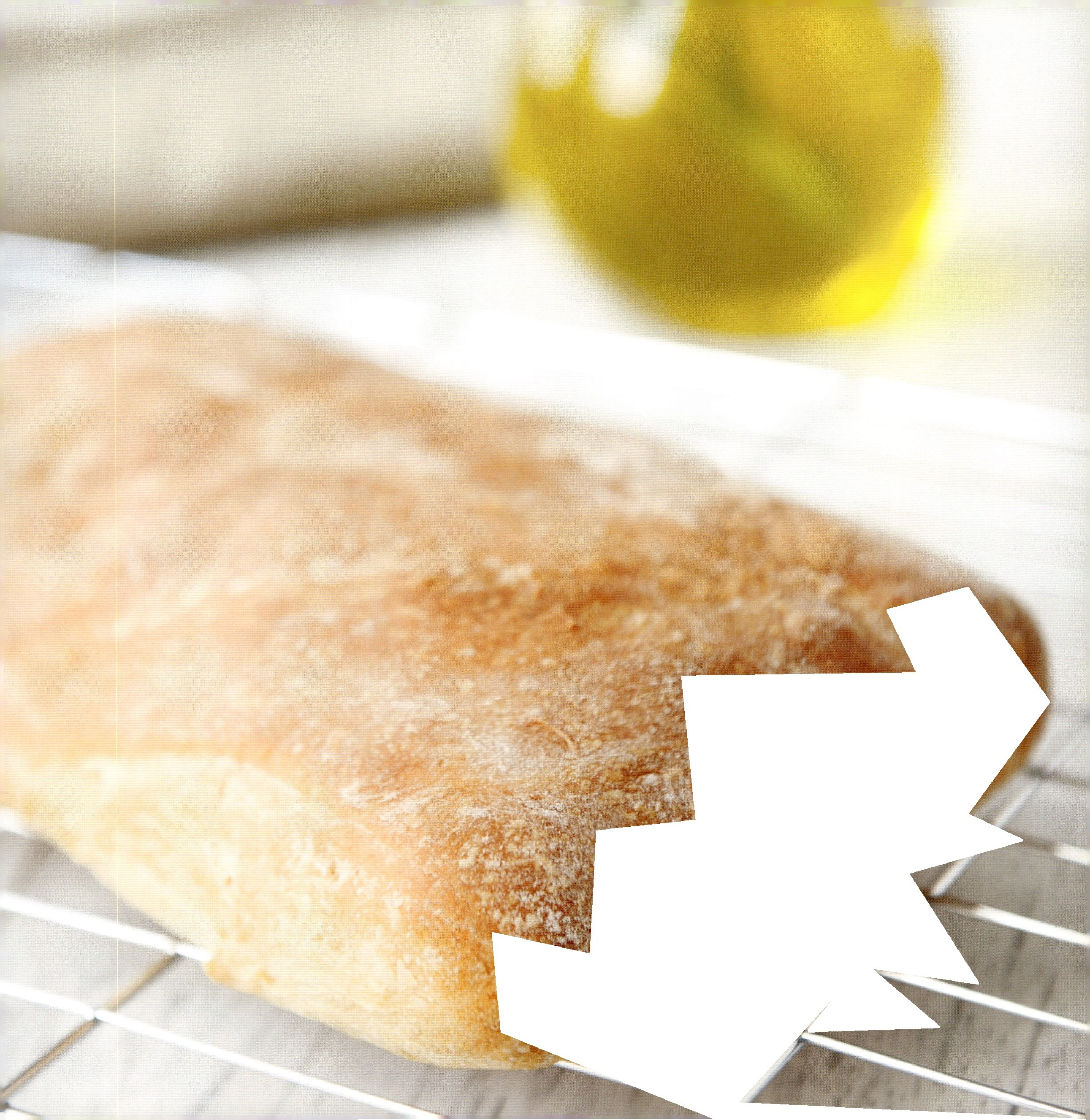

1 Mix together the ingredients for the pre-ferment in a bowl. Cover it with cling film (plastic wrap) and allow to develop either in a cool kitchen or in the fridge for at least 4 hours; preferably overnight. Once developed the pre-ferment should be bubbly and will have increased in volume.

2 Combine the pre-ferment with the additional flour, water, salt and yeast and work together into a fairly even dough in the bowl. Instead of turning out onto the surface and kneading this is best done in the bowl. Work the dough for 5 minutes.

3 Add 1 tablespoon of the olive oil to a clean bowl and add the dough. Take the outside edge of the dough, still in the bowl, and fold it in to the centre. Repeat this all the way around the bowl and then go round a second time folding in to the middle. This will start to work in the olive oil from the bowl. Pretty quickly the dough won't let you fold it in to the middle but will slip about as you try to do so. At this point cover it with cling film (plastic wrap) and set aside to rest for 1 hour.

4 After resting, add the second tablespoon of olive oil to the bowl on top of the dough and repeat the folding in to the middle. Cover again and rest for a further hour.

5 Fold in the rested dough once more, this time without adding any oil. Cover again and leave to rest this time for 15 minutes.

6 Prepare the work surface by dusting with a coating of flour: ciabatta dough requires a minimum of handling to retain the big air bubbles that will have started to form. You will also need three pieces of baking (parchment) paper cut into rectangles approximately 15 x 25cm (6 x 10in).

84 Perfect Pre-Ferment

7 Gently turn the dough out onto the flour and carefully stretch it out from the corners to form a large rectangle. Fold the left hand third into the middle, then the right hand third on top so that the sheet of dough is in 3 layers; this will create some strength in the finished loaves.

8 Using a sharp knife or dough blade split the folded rectangle into three equal pieces – these will form the finished loaves. Stretch them out gently and encourage each loaf to measure roughly 20 x 12cm (8 x 4¾in). Scoop up each loaf in turn and set one on each of the prepared pieces of baking paper. Set the loaves on their papers onto a flat baking sheet, cover and allow to rise for 1 hour in a warm spot.

9 Preheat the oven and a baking sheet to 210°C (fan)/230°C/450°F/Gas Mark 8. The preheated tray will create a big hit of heat for the loaves when they first go into the oven. When the loaves are ready to go in they should be blistered in places with large air bubbles. You need to treat them gently, no sharp knocks or those bubbles may burst!

10 Now prepare yourself for getting the loaves into the oven – you will need to slide each piece of paper and loaf onto the preheated tray in the oven in a quick movement. Ready? Let's go!

11 Bake the ciabatta for 20 minutes at the higher heat before reducing the temperature to 190°C (fan)/210°C/425°F/Gas Mark 7 and baking for a further 18 minutes. The high amount of moisture in the loaves mean that they need the full baking time otherwise they will soon soften on cooling – good Ciabatta have a crisp crust. Turning down the oven after the first 20 minutes will stop them from taking on too much colour while they finish baking. Transfer to a wire rack to cool.

Ciabatta with Olive Oil

ROSEMARY & SEA SALT FOCCACIA

A very popular Mediterranean bread with a chewy texture and drizzled with a good glug of olive oil. I've flavoured it simply with rosemary and sea salt but you could equally go to town with your favourite toppings.

MAKES 1 20 X 20CM (8 X 8IN) FOCCACIA
PREP 30 MINUTES PLUS 4 HOURS OR OVERNIGHT DEVELOPMENT OF THE PRE-FERMENT AND 3 HOURS 15 MINUTES PROVING | BAKE 25 MINUTES
OVEN 190°C (FAN)/210°C/425°F/GAS MARK 7

1. Use exactly the same method as the Ciabatta to create the Focaccia dough – the dough needs to be rested and turned in but without adding any extra olive oil.
2. When it is time to shape the dough, grease the 20cm (8in) square tin (pan). Add the dough to this and gently stretch it out into the corners to fill the tin evenly. Cover and set to one side for 1 hour to rise.
3. Once the dough is looking nicely puffy it is time to create the distinctive dimpled effect of focaccia. Measure out 1 tbsp olive oil into a small bowl. Dip your fingertips into the oil and poke the surface of the dough to create 'dimples'. Don't do it without oil on your fingers or you'll get stuck! Now drizzle over the oil from the bowl; the dimples will catch small pools of it.
4. Poke small sprigs of rosemary into the loaf, spaced evenly, and scatter the surface with the sea salt.
5. Bake in the oven for 25 minutes. Drizzle over the remaining 1 tbsp olive oil just before serving.

INGREDIENTS
Pre-Ferment
150g (5½oz) strong white bread flour
180ml/180g (6¼fl oz/6¼oz) water, cold
¼ tsp fast action yeast

Dough
325g (11½oz) strong white bread flour
175g/175ml (6fl oz/6 oz) water
1½ tsp salt
1 tsp yeast
1 tbsp olive oil
2 sprigs fresh rosemary
1 tsp sea salt

To serve
1 tbsp olive oil

EQUIPMENT
20 x 20cm (8 x 8in) baking tin (pan)

TIP
Foccacia can be left plain, simply drizzling with olive oil, or can be flavoured with your favourite ingredients; roasted peppers, sun-dried tomatoes, olives – the varieties are endless.

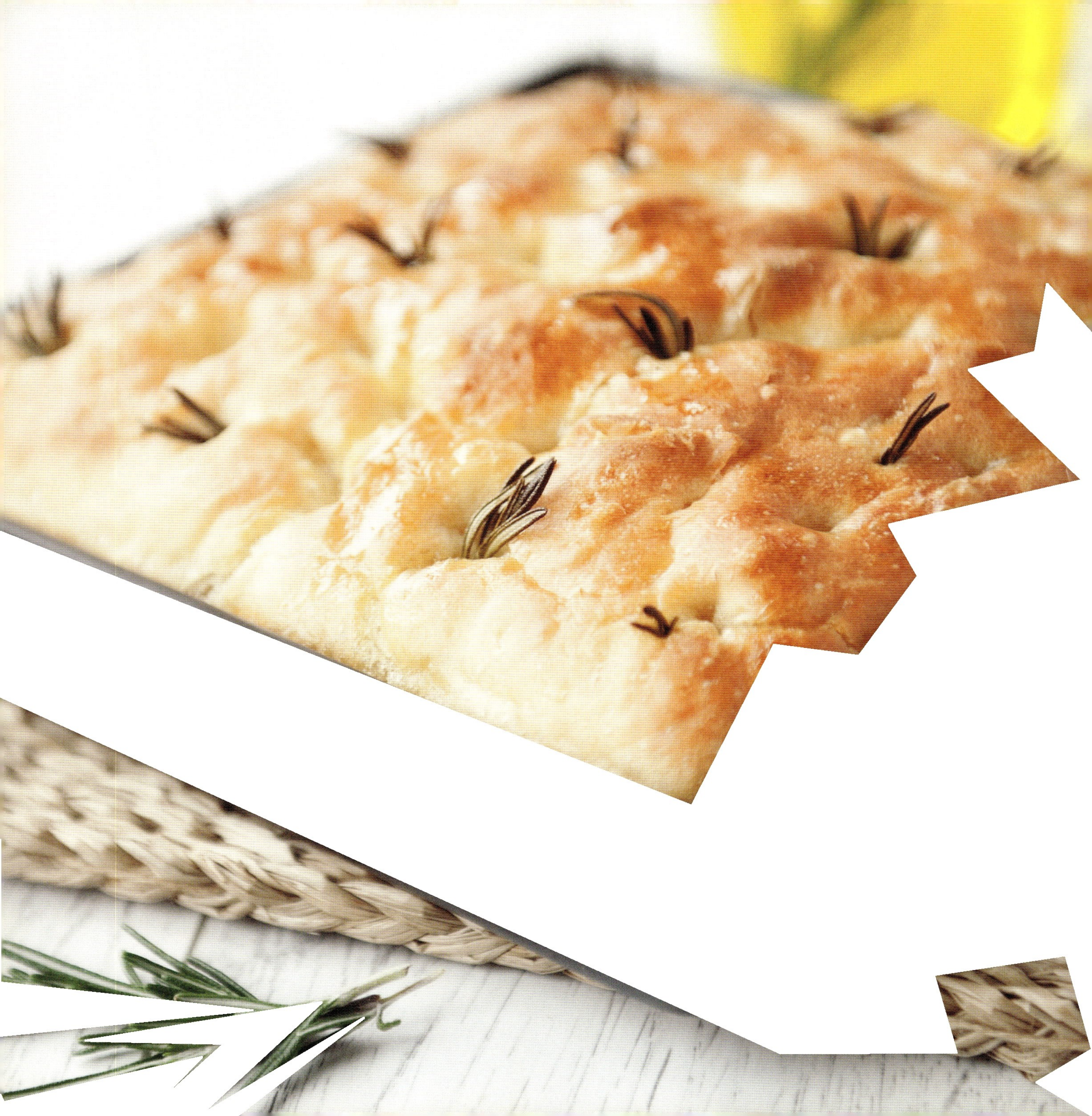

STILTON & CRANBERRY WHEEL

MAKES 1 ROUND LOAF
PREP ⏲ 35 MINUTES PLUS OVERNIGHT DEVELOPMENT OF THE
PRE-FERMENT AND 2 HOURS 15 MINUTES PROVING
BAKE ⏲ 20 MINUTES | OVEN 190°C (FAN)/210°C/425°F/GAS MARK 7

A tangy hit of Stilton cheese is the perfect match with plump dried cranberries – and, shaped into a wheel, this loaf is easy to break apart into portions for sharing.

INGREDIENTS
Pre-Ferment

50g (1¾oz) strong white bread flour

50g (1¾oz) wholemeal (whole wheat) bread flour

1 tsp fast action yeast

1 tsp malt extract

155ml/155g (5fl oz/5oz) water, cold

Dough

85g (3oz) strong white bread flour

50g (1¾oz) wholemeal (whole wheat) bread flour

¼ tsp salt

10g (¼oz) butter, diced and softened

25g (1oz) Stilton cheese

35g (1¼oz) dried cranberries

Oil for greasing

Glaze

1 egg, beaten

EQUIPMENT

Baking sheet

Rolling pin

Pastry brush

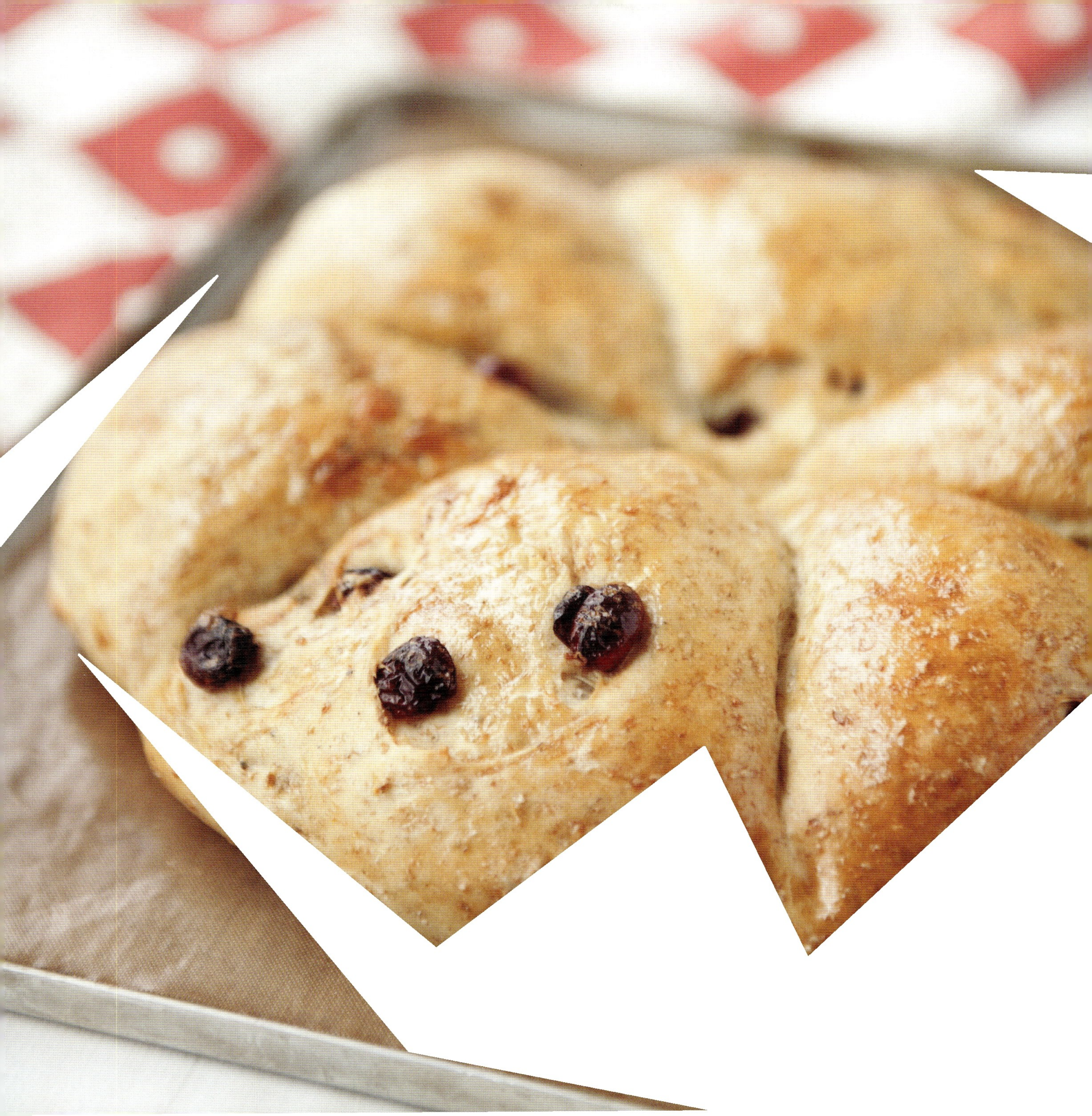

1 Mix the pre-ferment, stirring together the white and wholemeal (whole wheat) bread flours, yeast, malt extract and water in a bowl large enough to allow for the pre-ferment to rise. Cover with cling film (plastic wrap) and allow to develop in a cool kitchen or in the fridge for at least 4 hours; ideally overnight. Once developed the pre-ferment should be bubbly and will have increased in volume.

2 Add all the dough ingredients except the cheese and cranberries to the developed pre-ferment. Mix to a rough dough and then knead on the work surface for 10 minutes until smooth. This dough can be fairly sticky to work with so grease the surface and your hands with a little vegetable or sunflower oil. You need to keep reminding yourself that a sticky dough is not a bad thing and will provide you with a lovely tender loaf. Believe in the sticky dough!

3 Transfer the dough to a lightly oiled bowl, cover with cling film (plastic wrap) or a clean dish towel and allow to rise for 1½ hours or until doubled in size. Once risen, tip the dough out onto the work surface and knead lightly for two minutes to work out any large air bubbles.

4 Flatten the dough into a rough circle. Scatter over the dried cranberries and crumble over the stilton. Gather the dough together and knead lightly to distribute the cheese and fruit.

Perfect Pre-Ferment

5 Flatten the dough out into a rough circle once more and fold the edges inwards, repeating until they will fold no more to create the spine of the loaf. Flip it over so that the seam sits underneath. Cup both your hands around the ball and smooth them underneath the dough to tighten up the ball.

6 Now transfer the ball to a baking sheet lined with baking paper. A baking sheet without a lip is essential for the next stage of shaping. If you don't have one use a Swiss roll tin (jelly roll pan) but turn it upside down to bake on the flat side.

7 Lightly oil a rolling pin. Press this into the dough to create the distinctive 'wheel' spokes. Press down firmly but take care not to split the dough into pieces. Work three indents evenly across the loaf intersecting in the centre. To begin with the dough will spring back into place so you may need to go over the indents a couple of times.

8 Now the wheel is shaped, cover with a clean dish towel and set aside to rise for 45 minutes or until puffy and almost doubled in size. Preheat the oven to 190°C (fan)/210°C/425°F/Gas Mark 7. If the separations have closed up once the wheel is ready to bake, press in the indents with the length of your forefinger, brush well with beaten egg, and bake straight away in the preheated oven for 20 minutes. Transfer to a wire rack to cool completely.

Stilton & Cranberry Wheel

CHOCOLATE & HAZELNUT WHEEL

A sweet chocolate and hazelnut wheel in ready-made break-apart portions – good for eating on the go, as a snack or split and slathered with a good layer of chocolate spread!

MAKES 1 ROUND LOAF
PREP 35 MINUTES PLUS OVERNIGHT DEVELOPMENT OF THE PRE-FERMENT AND 2 HOURS 45 MINUTES PROVING | BAKE 20 MINUTES | OVEN 190°C (FAN)/210°C/425°F/GAS MARK 7

1. Make the pre-ferment in the same way as for the Stilton & Cranberry Wheel.

2. When it comes to turning the pre-ferment into dough, add caster sugar and cocoa powder (unsweetened cocoa) too. Knead and allow to rise until doubled in size. The addition of cocoa makes this dough take slightly longer than the Stilton & Cranberry version and will take about 2 hours to double in size.

3. After knocking back the dough work in the chocolate chunks and roughly chopped hazelnuts. Shape into a wheel as described in the Stilton & Cranberry Wheel. Allow to rise again until almost doubled in size. Brush with beaten egg and scatter over the finely chopped hazelnuts. Bake in the oven for 20 minutes. Allow to cool on a wire rack and serve.

INGREDIENTS
Pre-Ferment
50g (1¾oz) strong white bread flour
50g (1¾oz) wholemeal (whole wheat) bread flour
1 tsp fast action yeast
1 tsp malt extract
155ml/155g (5fl oz/5oz) water, cold

Dough
85g (3oz) strong white bread flour
50g (1¾oz) wholemeal (whole wheat) bread flour
¼ tsp salt
15g (½oz) caster (superfine) sugar
2 tsp cocoa powder (unsweetened cocoa)
10g (¼oz) butter, diced and softened
30g (1oz) milk chocolate chunks
25g blanched hazelnuts, roughly chopped
1 tbsp blanched hazelnuts, finely chopped
Oil for greasing

Glaze
1 egg, beaten

EQUIPMENT
Baking sheet
Rolling pin
Pastry brush

TIP Take care when shaping the wheel by indenting the divisions not to split the dough, press firmly but not right the way down to the baking sheet below.

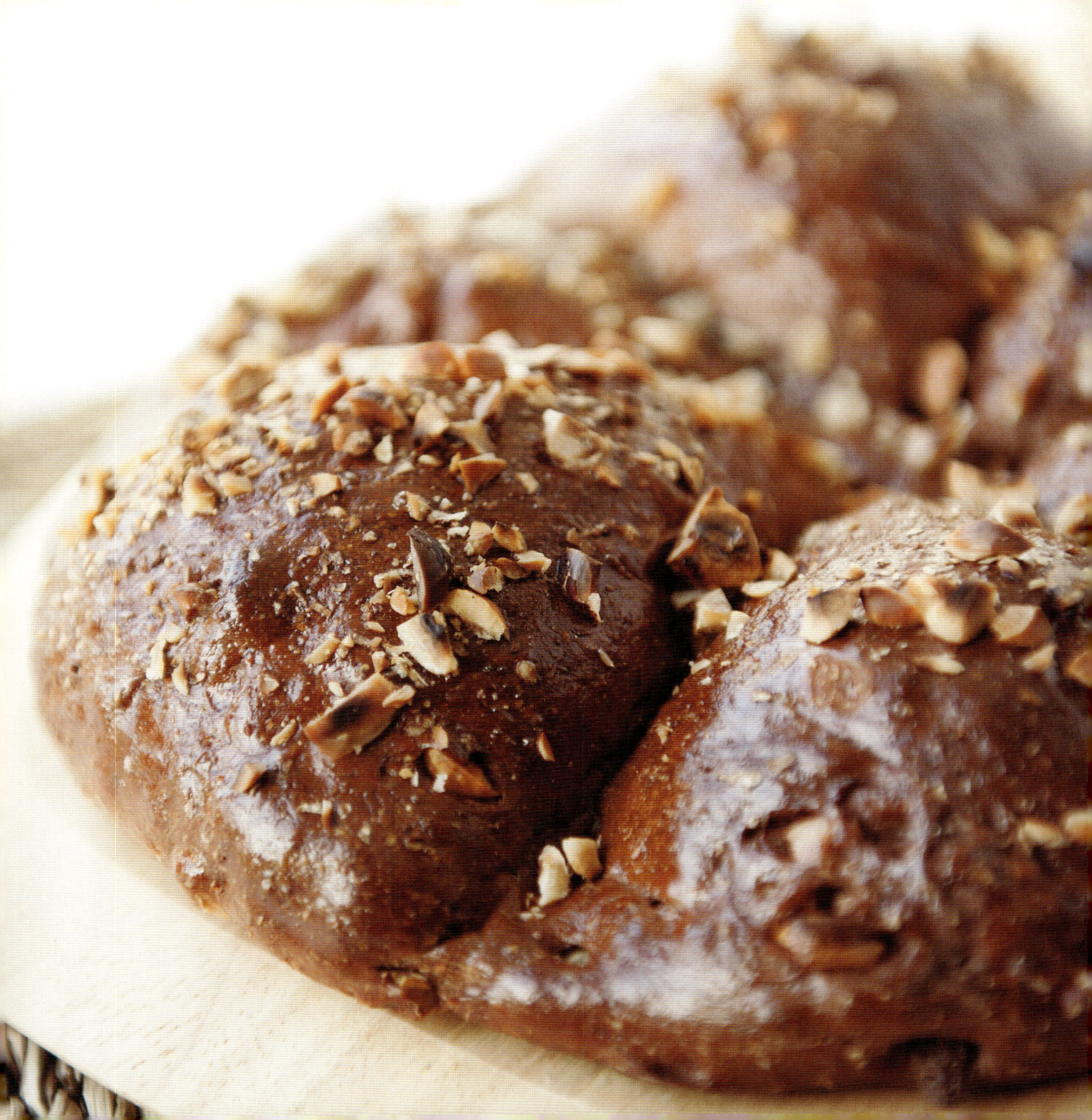

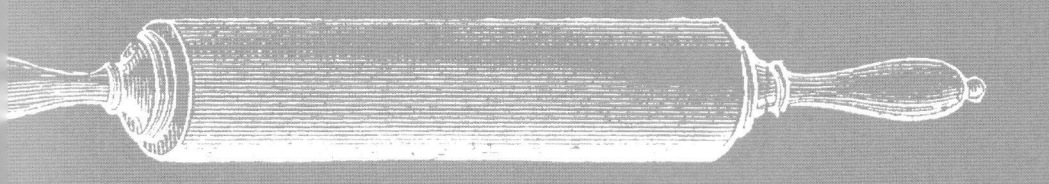

FURTHER FAVOURITES

Recipes in this section have slightly different methods from regular doughs. This doesn't mean they're difficult though; follow the step-by-step instructions and you'll soon be on your way to baking success!

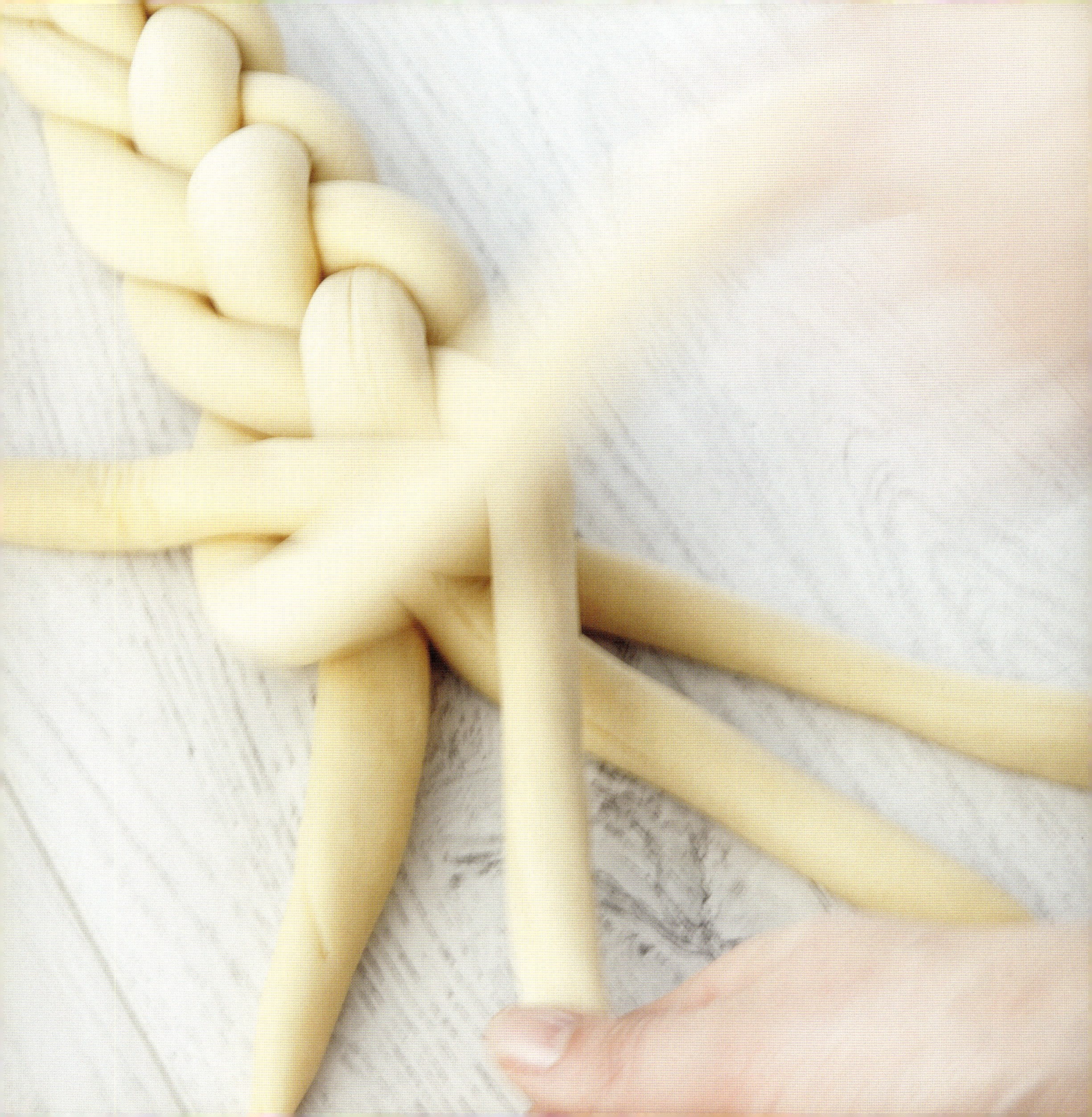

BAGELS

MAKES 8 BAGELS
PREP ⏰ 45 MINUTES PLUS 1½ HOURS PROVING
BAKE ⏰ 20 MINUTES
OVEN 190°C (FAN)/210°C/425°F/GAS MARK 7

Bagels are fun to make if you fancy a bit of 'different' bread making. The key to chewy bagels lies in the poaching so don't be tempted to miss this step out – and don't be daunted, you'll soon be poaching and baking bagels like a pro.

INGREDIENTS

Dough

450g (1lb) strong white bread flour
1½ tsp fast action yeast
1½ tsp salt
20g (¾oz) caster sugar
48ml/45g (1¾fl oz/1½oz) vegetable or sunflower oil
225ml/225g (8fl oz/8oz) lukewarm water
Oil for greasing

Coating

1 tbsp malt extract for poaching
1 egg, beaten
2 tbsp poppy seeds
2 tbsp sesame seeds

EQUIPMENT

Large baking sheet
Large pan
Fish slice/slotted spoon
Dish towel
Pastry brush

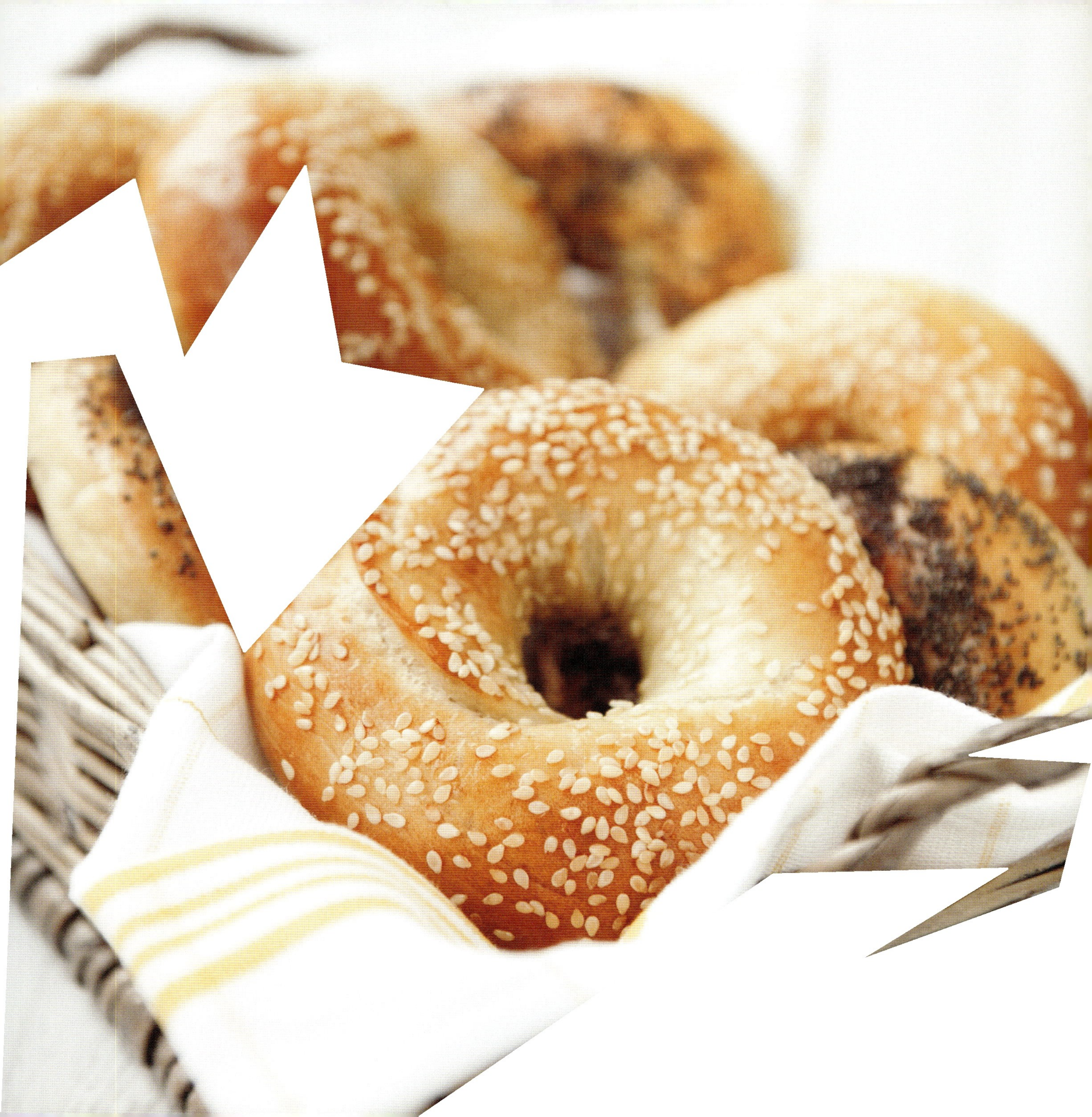

1. To make the dough measure the dry ingredients into a large mixing bowl. Make a well in the centre and pour in the water and oil. Combine the ingredients together to form a rough dough.

2. Tip the dough out onto the work surface and knead for 10 minutes. Transfer the dough to an oiled bowl, cover and allow it to rise for 1 hour or until doubled in size.

TIP
Try adding half a chopped and gently fried onion to the dough to create onion bagels. The onion will increase the amount of time the dough takes to rise and double in size so allow a little extra time.

3. Knead the dough lightly on the work surface and then split it into 8 equal-sized pieces. By eye is fine unless you want to be exact – weigh the full dough on the scales and divide by 8 to give you a weight for each piece of dough. Grease a large baking sheet.

4. Take the first piece of dough and roll it into a sausage shape, rolling the dough back and forth over the work surface with the palm of your hand. This will create a bone-shaped piece of dough.

Further Favourites

5 Now use both palms, placing one over each bulbous end, to roll an even-shaped piece of dough. Keep the pressure firm and even.

TIP Dough can be awkward when you are trying to lengthen it. If it is resisting, let it rest for a couple of minutes before trying again. This allows the dough to relax so that you can continue to shape it easily.

6 Roll the sausage to approximately 25cm long and taper the ends slightly by applying more pressure. Curl the dough round into a ring to form the bagel, joining the two tapered ends together with a 4cm (1½in) overlap. Pinch the seal together well to avoid it coming apart. Transfer to the baking sheet.

Bagels

7 Repeat steps 4–6 to shape the remaining bagels, cover them with a clean dish towel and allow to prove for 30 minutes until nicely puffed up. Preheat the oven to 190ºC (fan)/210°C/425°F/Gas Mark 7.

8 Bring a large pan of water to the boil and add 1 tablespoon of malt extract. Don't go out and buy it especially – if you have it, great, if not use 1 tablespoon of caster sugar. Turn the heat down so the water is at a very gentle simmer.

TIP
Be sure to keep the pan of poaching liquid on the heat on a very low simmer. If the water is allowed to cool too much then the outside surface of the bagels will not poach correctly and they will stick to the dish towel as you drain them!

9 Now it's time to poach the bagels. Do it in batches depending on how many you can fit in the pan of water. Lay out a clean dish towel on the work surface and have a fish slice or slotted spoon to hand. Quickly but carefully place the first batch of bagels into the pan of simmering water. Poach them for 1 minute on each side, flipping them carefully over in the water with the fish slice.

10 Remove from the pan with the fish slice, supporting the join as you do so. Set them on the dish towel to drain and poach the remainder.

11 Transfer the poached bagels to the greased baking sheet. Brush liberally with the beaten egg, then sprinkle with the poppy and sesame seeds.

12 Bake in the preheated oven for 20 minutes until golden. Once baked transfer to a wire rack to cool completely.

TIP
Poach 2–3 bagels at a time, don't overload the pan or you won't have enough room to flip them over mid-poach!

Bagels

SWEET CINNAMON & CRANBERRY BAGELS

Sweet cinnamon bagels – a great snack any time of the day and ideal for splitting and toasting for breakfast.

MAKES 8 BAGELS
PREP 45 MINUTES PLUS 1½ HOURS PROVING
BAKE 20 MINUTES
OVEN 190°C (FAN)/210°C/425°F/GAS MARK 7

INGREDIENTS
Dough
450g (1lb) strong white bread flour
1½ tsp fast action yeast
1 tsp salt
50g (1¾oz) caster sugar
2 tsp ground cinnamon
48ml/45g (1¾fl oz/1½oz) vegetable or sunflower oil
235ml/235g (8¼fl oz/8¼oz) lukewarm water
Oil for greasing
70g (2½oz) dried cranberries

Coating
1tbsp malt extract, for poaching
1 egg, beaten

EQUIPMENT
Large pan
Slotted spoon/fish slice
Dish towel
Pastry brush
Large baking sheet

1. The method for making the sweet bagels is the same as the savoury version but add the cinnamon along with the flour. They also need a little more water when it comes to making the dough. Incorporate the dried cranberries in the dough after the first rise, kneading until they are evenly dispersed.

2. Shaping the dough sausages is a little more tricky as the cranberries try to burst out of the dough – if they do just poke them back in until the sausage of dough is shaped the way you want it.

3. Allow the shaped bagels to double in size on the greased baking sheet, poach in simmering water with 1tbsp malt extract added, glaze with beaten egg and then bake for 20 minutes in the oven.

TIP
Only glaze the bagels directly before baking. If the glaze is allowed to sit in the open air it dries out and won't provide the glossy golden effect you're looking for.

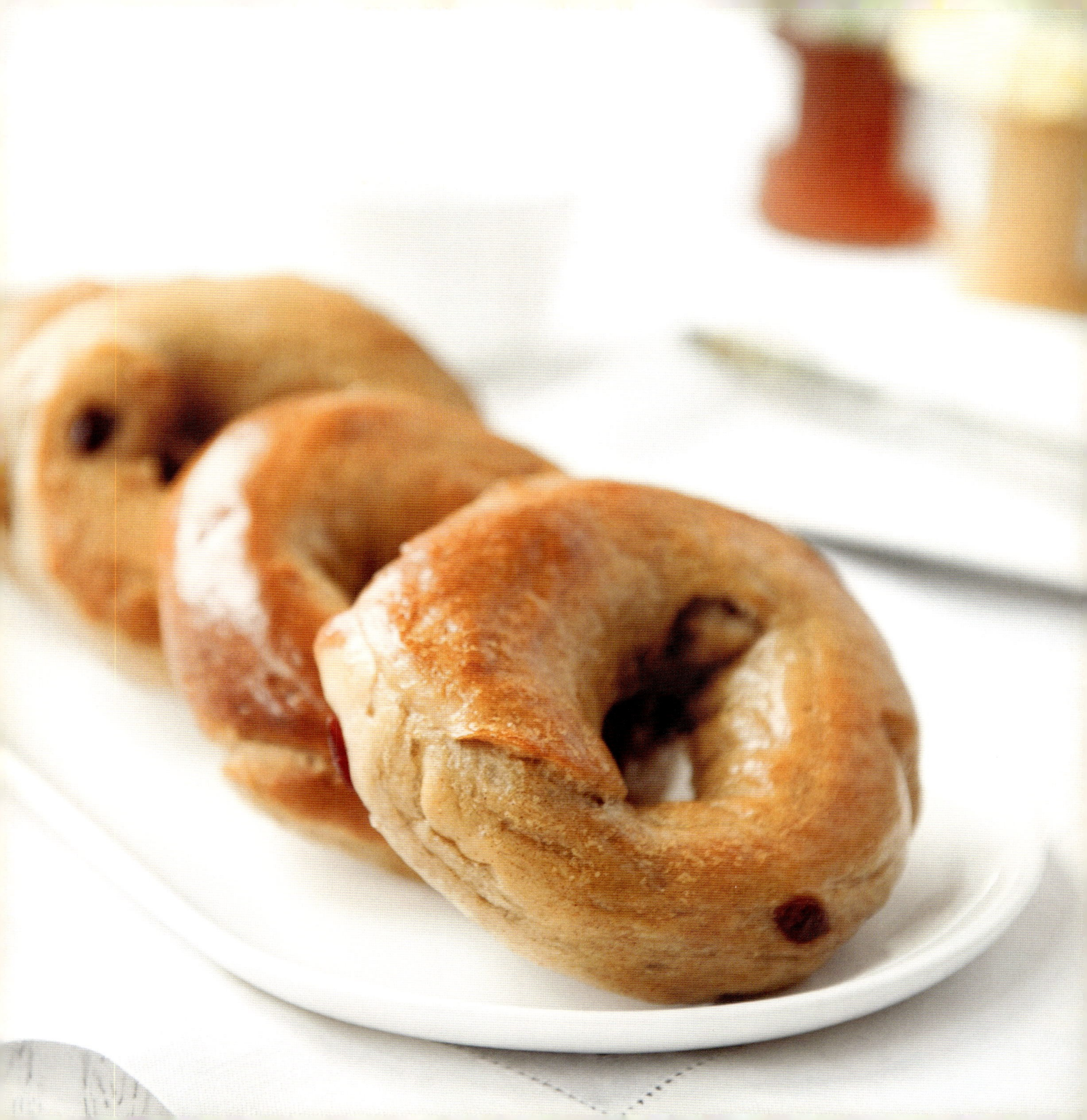

CHALLAH

MAKES 1 BRAIDED LOAF
PREP 🕐 **45 MINUTES PLUS OVERNIGHT PROVING AND 2 HOURS PROVING**
BAKE 🕐 **30 MINUTES | OVEN 190°C (FAN)/210°C/425°F/GAS MARK 7 THEN 160°C (FAN)/180°C/350°F/GAS MARK 4**

Braiding strands of dough into a loaf isn't difficult, as long as you have the right kind of dough to work with. This Challah dough, enriched with egg and oil, is perfect for the job: a firm dough that is just the right consistency for rolling into strands and braiding, and firm enough to hold its shape on rising. And don't worry, there are full instructions for the braiding!

INGREDIENTS
Bread
490g (1lb 1½oz) strong white bread flour
40g (1½oz) sugar
2 egg yolks, large
1 egg, large
40ml/37g (1½fl oz/1¼oz) vegetable oil
160ml/160g (5¾fl oz/5¾oz) water, cold
1½ tsp salt
1½ tsp fast action yeast
Oil for greasing

Glaze
1 egg, beaten

EQUIPMENT
Large baking sheet
Pastry brush

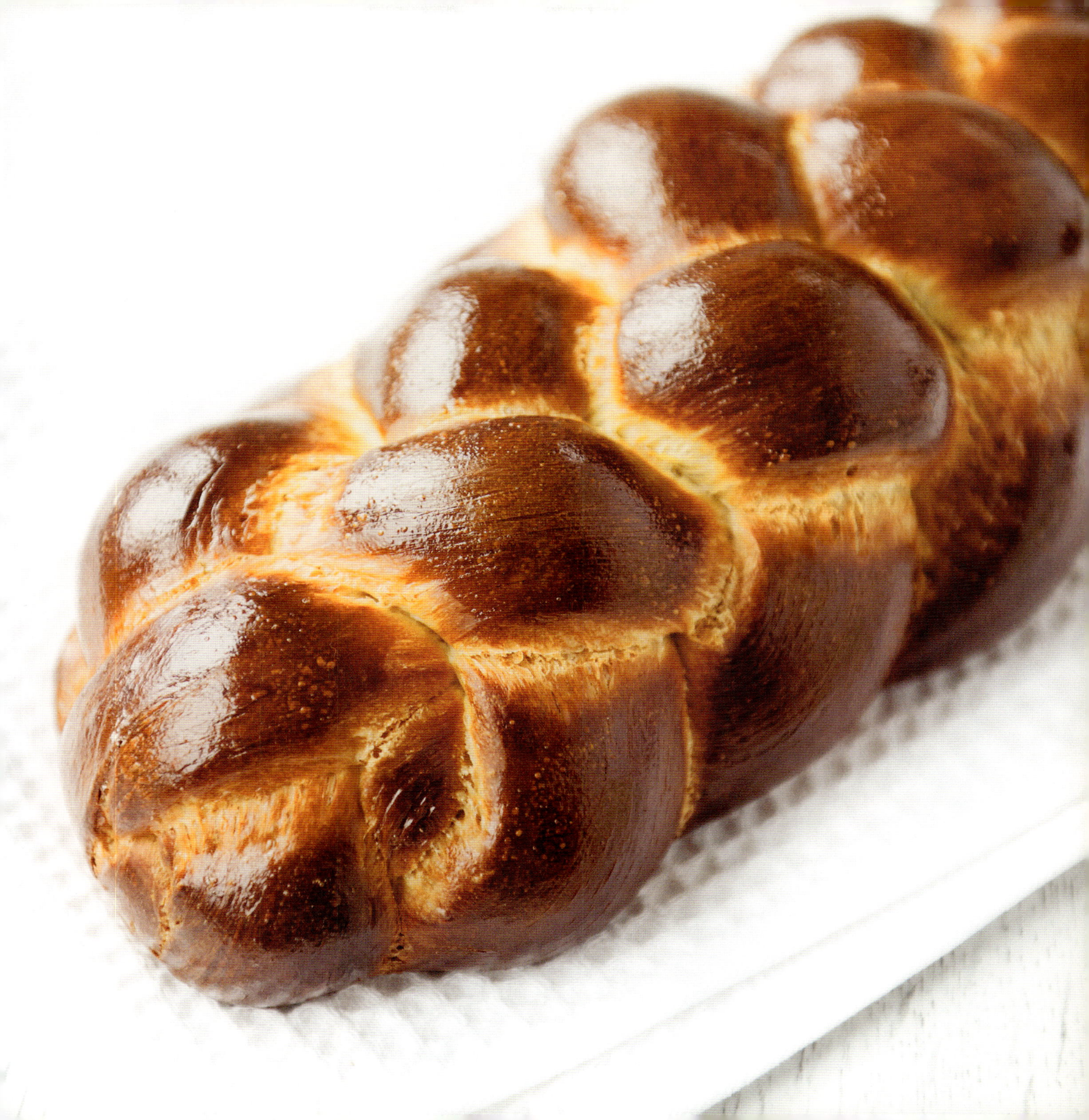

1 Place all the bread ingredients into a large bowl and combine to form a rough dough. Turn out onto the work surface and knead for 8 minutes, stretching and folding the dough. The dough will be firm and you'll need to use a bit more effort than usual to knead it effectively.

2 Transfer the smooth (though still a little tight) dough to a lightly oiled bowl. Cover with cling film (plastic wrap) and allow to rise overnight in the fridge.

3 The next morning remove the dough from the fridge: it will have almost doubled in size overnight. Turn it out onto the work surface and split it into 6 equal portions.

4 Working with one piece at a time, flatten the dough out and then fold the edges in to the centre, and flip it over so that the seam sits underneath. Shape it into a rough ball by placing your hand over the top, then bend your fingers around to form a sort of cage over the dough. Lightly turn the dough in your hand by rotating it with your fingertips and it will soon be a ball shape.

5 Take a ball of dough and roll it between your palm and the work surface to start to elongate it. You won't get far before it feels impossible and it keeps shrinking back in size – about 10cm (4in). Set it aside at this point and shape another portion.

TIP
Keep it slow and steady when rolling the strands – as soon as the dough starts to fight back, set it to one side and roll another portion.

6 By the time you've shaped each ball, the first portion of dough will have relaxed enough to roll out once more. Roll it again between your palm and the work surface to elongate the strand. When the dough starts springing back again set it to one side and work through the other five strands.

7 Keep going in this manner and eventually you will be rolling the strand between both hands and the work surface, moving your hands outwards to stretch the dough. You're aiming for a length of around 40cm (15¾in) with slightly tapered ends. The thickest part of the strand in the middle should be about 2cm (¾in) wide.

Challah 107

Arm 1   Arm 2

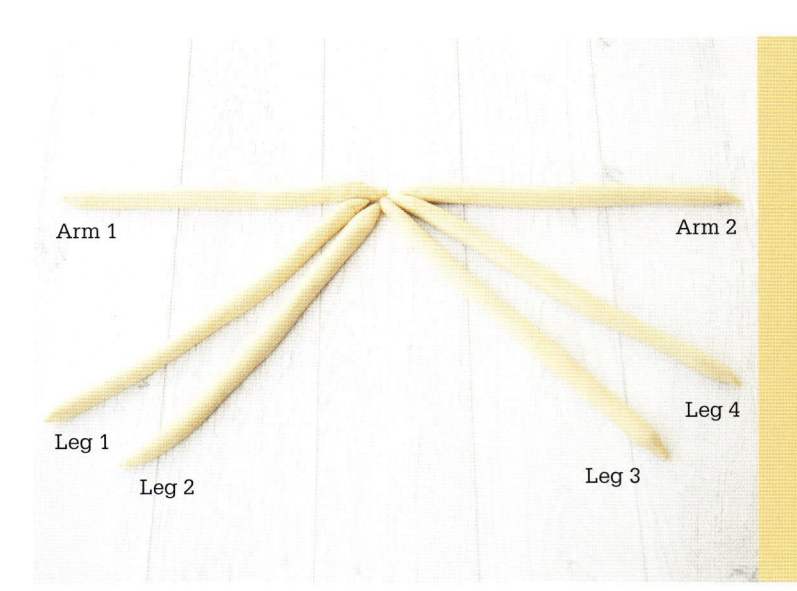

Leg 1

Leg 2   Leg 3

Leg 4

8 Once all six strands are rolled out to the same size and length it's time for the braiding. Make sure you've enough space to work in. We'll do it together, one step at a time. Line up the six strands as follows: One horizontally to the left, one horizontally to the right – we'll call these arms. Two legs point down to the left, two legs down to the right leaving a space in the middle. All the strands should sit side by side at a centre point at the top. Pinch together the strands at the centre point to secure them together, press the dough down onto the work surface to stick it there.

9 Move arm 1 from the left down into the middle of the legs. Move arm 2 across to replace arm 1.

10 Leg 1 on the far left moves up to form the arm on the right.

108   Further Favourites

11 Now it's just a case of repeating the following movements until you reach the ends of the strands:

Arm 1 to the middle of the legs.
Far right leg moves up to replace Arm 1.
Arm 2 to the middle of the legs.
Far left leg moves up to replace Arm 2.

12 It gets a little tricky as the strands get short. Braid until you can braid no more, pinch together the dough at the end and fold underneath to neaten it up. Release the dough at the top of the braid where it was secured to the surface and fold that underneath the loaf too. There – aren't you proud?

13 Transfer the braid to a baking sheet lined with baking (parchment) paper, cover with a clean dish towel and allow to rise for 2 hours. Preheat the oven to 190°C (fan)/210°C/425°F/Gas Mark 7.

14 Double glaze the risen braid with beaten egg: this will give it its characteristic shine. Bake in the preheated oven for 10 minutes, then reduce the heat to 160°C (fan)/180°C/350°F/Gas Mark 4 and bake for a further 20 minutes. Allow to cool on a wire rack.

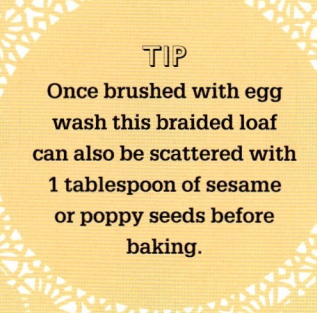

TIP
Once brushed with egg wash this braided loaf can also be scattered with 1 tablespoon of sesame or poppy seeds before baking.

Challah

HERBY BRAIDED LOAF

A fragrant braided loaf flavoured with your favourite fresh herb combination. Finely chopped herbs flavour the Challah dough wonderfully without any chunky additions that would make rolling strands and braiding difficult.

MAKES 1 BRAIDED LOAF
PREP ⏱ 45 MINUTES PLUS OVERNIGHT PROVING AND 2 HOURS PROVING
BAKE ⏱ 10 MINUTES | OVEN 190°C (FAN)/210°C/425°F/GAS MARK 7 THEN 160°C (FAN)/180°C/350°F/GAS MARK 4

INGREDIENTS

490g (1lb 1½oz) strong white bread flour
40g (1½oz) sugar
2 egg yolks, large
1 egg, large
40ml/37g (1½fl oz/1¼oz) vegetable oil
160ml/160g (5¾fl oz/5¾oz) water, cold
1½ tsp salt
1½ tsp fast action yeast
5 tbsp fresh mixed herbs such as basil, oregano, parsley and tarragon, finely chopped
Oil for greasing

Glaze

1 egg, beaten

EQUIPMENT

Pastry brush
Large baking sheet

Follow the Challah method but add 5 tablespoons of finely chopped fresh herbs to the bowl of ingredients before mixing to a rough dough.

TIP
This dough may feel a little softer than regular Challah after its overnight proving. This is due to the herbs releasing oil and flavouring the dough.

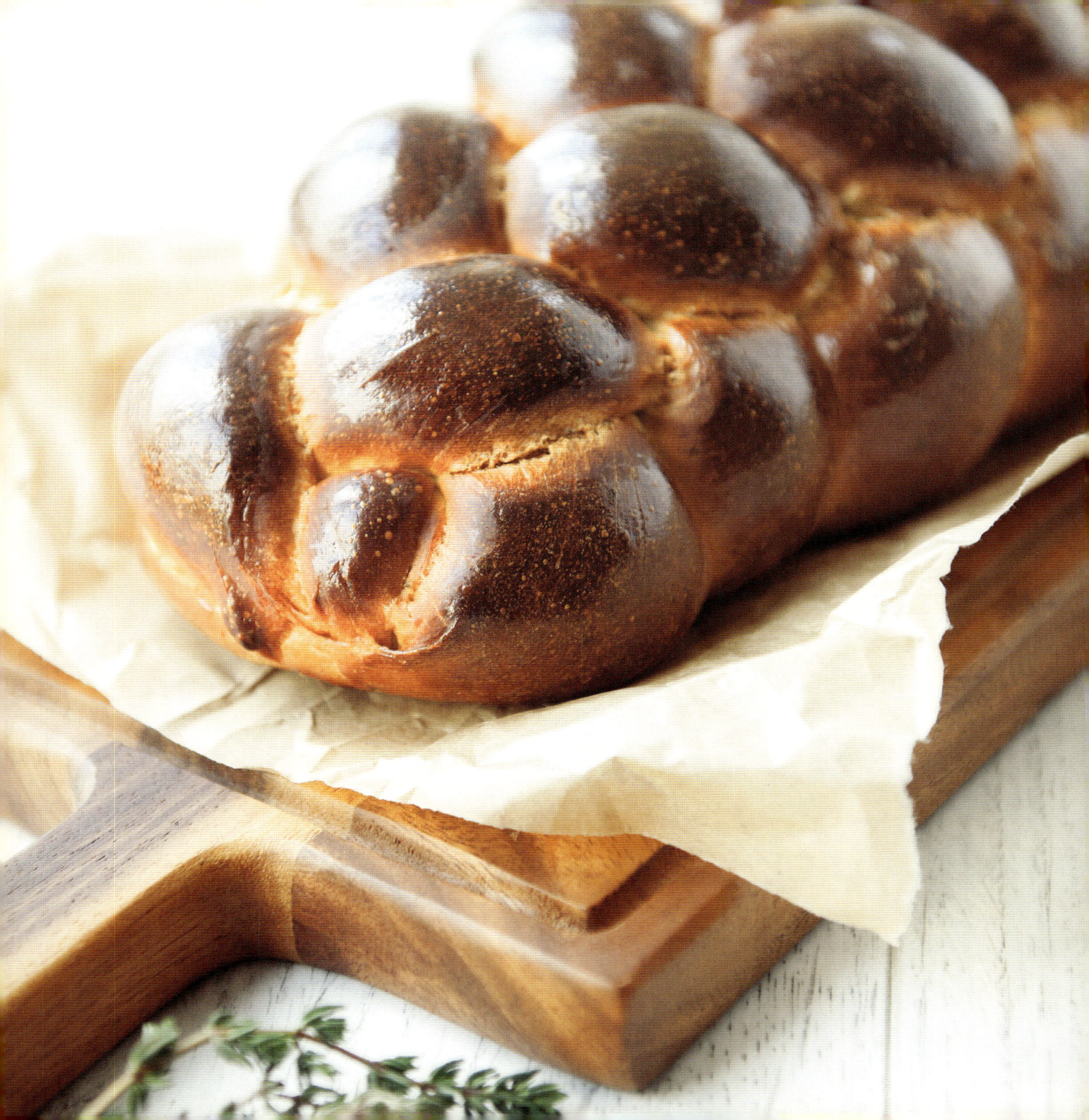

BRIOCHE

MAKES 1 LARGE TIN (PAN) LOAF
PREP 25 MINUTES PLUS 6 HOURS PROVING
BAKE 40 MINUTES | OVEN 160°C (FAN)/180°C/350°F/GAS MARK 4

A deliciously buttery bread, enriched with eggs and notorious for being tricky, sticky and everything in between! This is a dough that is best kneaded in a stand mixer if you have one. The method is simplified from a traditional brioche method but will still deliver fantastic results. Leftover Brioche makes wonderful bread and butter pudding.

INGREDIENTS

250g (9oz) strong white bread flour
30g (1oz) caster (superfine) sugar
2 eggs, large
2 tsp water, cold
½ tsp salt
1½ tsp fast action yeast
125g (4½oz) butter, softened

Glaze

1 egg, beaten

EQUIPMENT

Stand mixer
900g (2lb) loaf tin (pan)
Pastry brush
Baking sheet

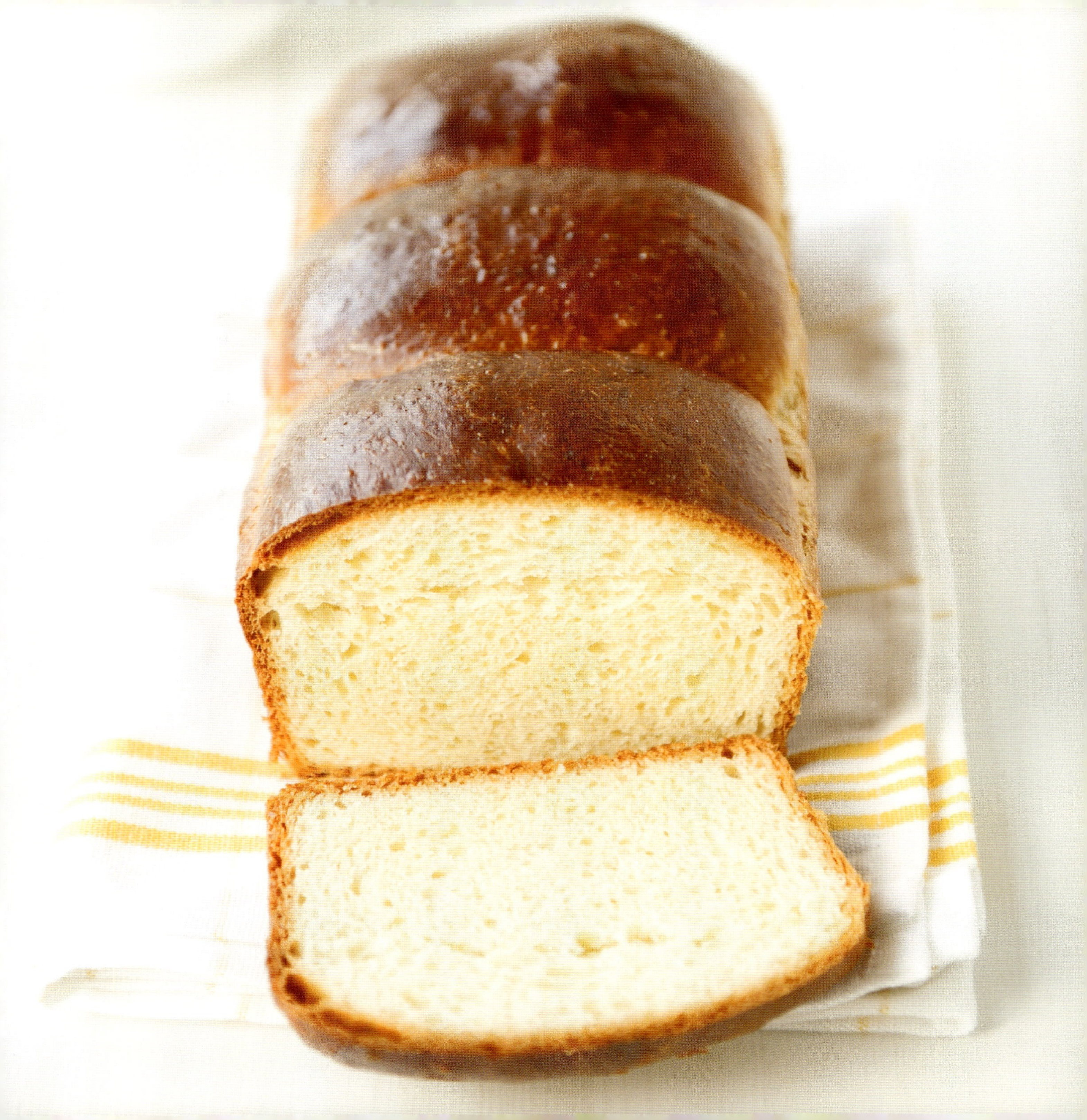

1. Place all the ingredients into the bowl of a stand mixer and fit the normal cake making beater, not the dough hook. This dough starts off much more like a cake batter and the dough hook just can't catch and mix it.

TIP If you are making the dough by hand, mix the ingredients in a large bowl with your hand shaped like a claw.

2. Turn on the mixer and get it beating the dough together. Let it mix for 5 minutes. To begin with it will look like a bread dough gone wrong, then after a little mixing it will start to look like a creamed butter and sugar mixture as it starts to stick to the sides of the bowl.

3. After five minutes the dough will be looking much smoother, clinging to the sides of the bowl and you will see strands forming in the dough. Stop the mixer and scrape the dough down into a ball that sits in the base of the bowl.

TIP
10 minutes' kneading on the work surface if making the dough by hand – it will be very sticky but you've come this far so persevere!

4. Change the beater for the dough hook and allow the mixer to knead the dough at speed 2 for 10 minutes.

114 Further Favourites

5 Transfer the dough to a clean bowl, cover and allow to rise at room temperature for 1 hour. After 1 hour place the bowl of dough in the fridge to rise for a further 2 hours. This chills the dough sufficiently so that it can be shaped.

6 Split the dough into three equal pieces. Flatten each portion on the work surface and fold the outside edges in to the centre. Flip the dough over. Shape it into a rough ball by placing your hand over the top, then bend your fingers around to form a cage over the dough. Lightly turn the dough in your hand by rotating it with your fingertips and it will soon be a ball shape.

7 Set the three balls into the loaf tin, cover and allow to rise for 2–3 hours until they have filled out and almost reach the top of the tin.

TIP
The chilled Brioche dough will be firm and a little clay-like but it means that it can easily be shaped into balls without ending up in a sticky mess. Because it's cold it will rise slowly.

8 Preheat the oven to 160°C (fan)/180°C/350°F/Gas Mark 4 and position one shelf at the top of the oven and one about two thirds of the way down.

9 Brush the top of the loaf with beaten egg to glaze and place the loaf on the lower shelf to bake for 40 minutes. At the same time put a baking sheet onto the top shelf. The sheet will prevent the top of the loaf from browning too much and should go in at the same time as the loaf. Once baked, carefully remove the loaf from the tin (pan) and set on a wire rack to cool completely.

Brioche

BRIOCHE PIZZA

Pizzas aren't the first thing you think about making when it comes to brioche dough, but once you try it I'm pretty sure you'll be converted. Use the suggestions or go with your own favourite toppings.

MAKES 2 X 20CM (8IN) PIZZAS
PREP 25 MINUTES PLUS 6 HOURS PROVING
BAKE 15-18 MINUTES
OVEN 180°C (FAN)/200°C/400°F/GAS MARK 6

TIP
One quantity of dough will make 2 pizzas. The dough can easily be frozen once portioned, wrapped in a freezer bag.

INGREDIENTS
250g (9oz) strong white bread flour
30g (1oz) caster (superfine) sugar
2 eggs, large
2 tsp water, cold
½ tsp salt
1½ tsp fast action yeast
125g (4½oz) butter, softened

TOPPING
200g (7oz) cherry tomatoes, halved
150g (5½oz) mozzarella, sliced
Small handful basil leaves

EQUIPMENT
Stand mixer
2 baking sheets

1. Prepare the dough as for the Brioche. Split the chilled dough into two equal portions.

2. Roll out the dough into two 20cm (8in) circles and transfer each to a well-greased baking sheet. Cover and allow to rise for 1½ hours until puffy.

3. Add the pizza topping, leaving 2cm (¾in) of dough clear all the way around the edge of each pizza.

4. Bake in a preheated the oven for 15–18 minutes, until the dough is golden and the topping is piping hot. Serve.

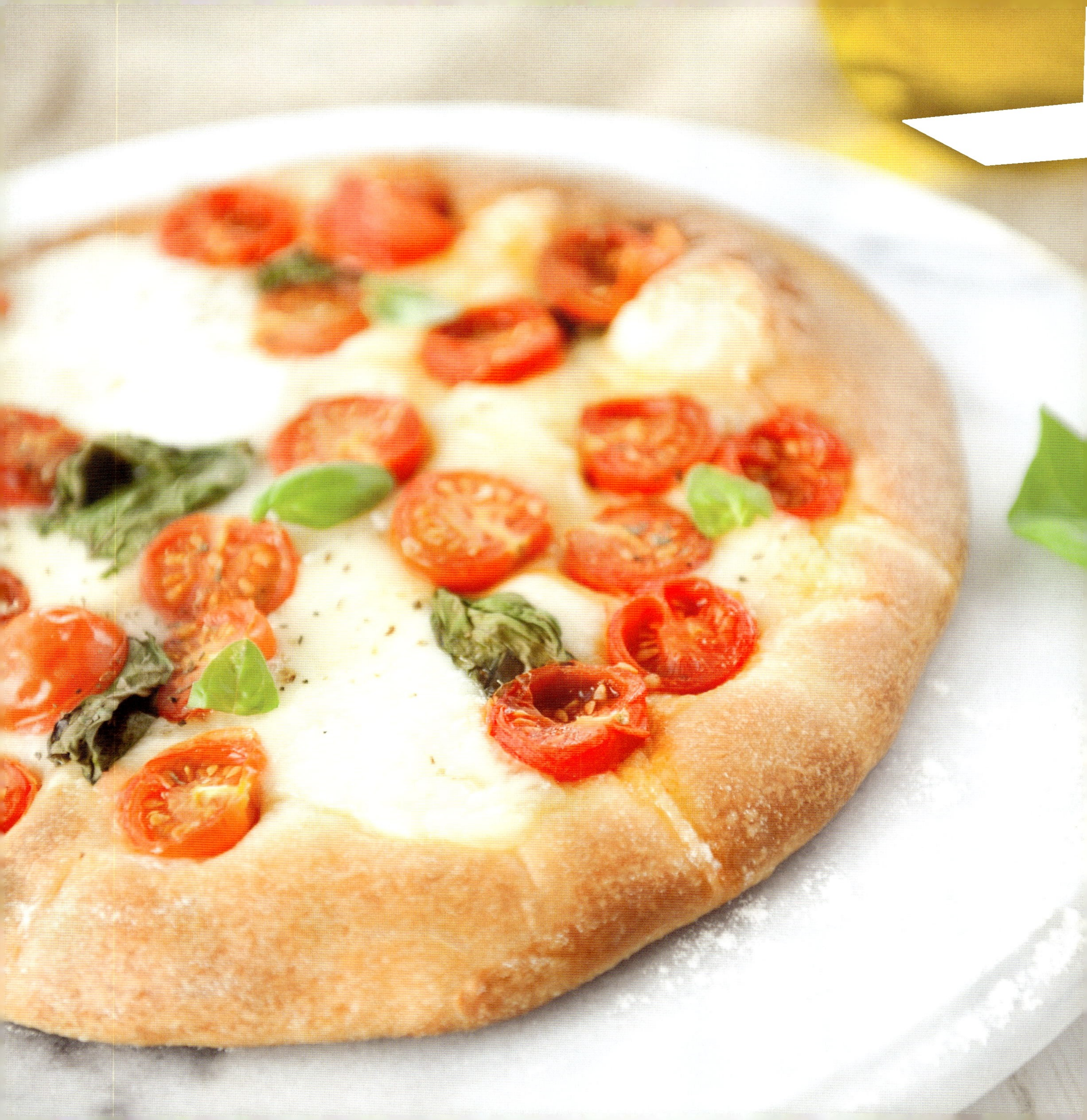

DANISH PASTRY – RAISIN WHIRLS

MAKES 8 WHIRLS USING A HALF PORTION OF DANISH PASTRY
PREP 🕐 **DANISH PASTRY – 35 MINUTES PLUS 4 HOURS OR OVERNIGHT RESTING**
RAISIN WHIRLS – 15 MINUTES PLUS 2½ HOURS PROVING
BAKE 🕐 **12 MINUTES | OVEN 190°C (FAN)/210°C/425°F/GAS MARK 7**

There's nothing more satisfying than the smell (and taste!) of a freshly baked Danish pastry. They aren't difficult to make, but you need to plan in advance. The pastry, once made, keeps well in the fridge for up to three days and can be frozen in half portions to use at a later date.

INGREDIENTS
Danish Pastry

350g (12oz) strong white bread flour

40g (1½oz) caster (superfine) sugar

1½ tsp fast action yeast

250g (9oz) butter, cold, cut into thin sticks

125ml/129g (4½fl oz / 45/8oz) milk

50ml/50g (1¾fl oz / 1¾oz) water, cold

1 egg, large

Filling

150g (5½oz) raisins

40g (1½oz) currants

200ml/200g (7fl oz/7oz) boiling water

25g (1oz) light muscovado sugar

½ tsp mixed spice

Glaze

1 egg, beaten

EQUIPMENT
Food processor

Rolling pin

Sieve

Serrated bread knife

2 baking sheets

Cling film (plastic wrap)

Pastry brush

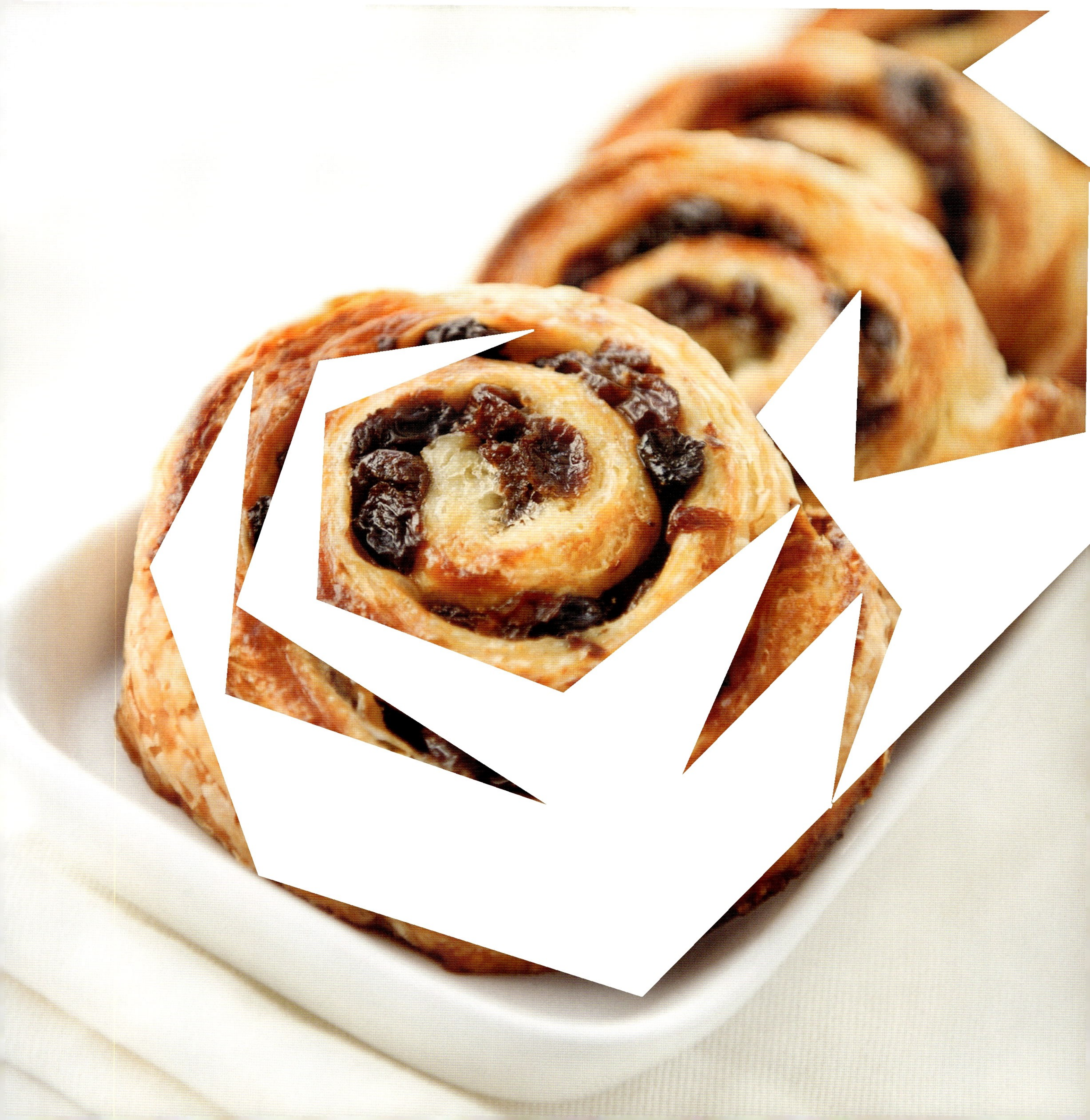

DANISH PASTRY

1. Place the flour, sugar and dried yeast into the bowl of a food processor and give it a quick blitz to mix evenly. Add the butter and blitz again, until the butter is broken up into pebble-like chunks.

2. Tip the mixture out into a large bowl and make a well in the centre. Measure the milk and water into a jug and add the egg. Whisk well.

3. Pour the liquid into the dry ingredients and combine together using a table knife. It will be fairly sticky and speckled with the butter. Gather the dough together into a ball, wrap well in cling film (plastic wrap) and place It in the fridge for 4 hours or overnight.

4. Flour the work surface and unwrap the chilled pastry. Roll out the dough into a long thin rectangle, 20 x 50cm (8 x 20in), keeping the rolling pin and surface lightly dusted with flour. If a blob of butter breaks through add a dab of flour to its surface to keep it in place. Fold the bottom third of the rectangle up and the top third down in an envelope style fold.

5. Turn the folded dough 90 degrees so that the folds are now left and right. Repeat the rolling and folding in step 4 a further 3 times. If the dough becomes difficult to roll out let it rest for 5–10 minutes before rolling again. That's the Danish pastry done. Each of the recipes (Raisin Whirls and Croissants) use a half block of dough so cut it in half and wrap each portion in cling film (plastic wrap). These can be kept in the fridge or frozen for up to a month for later use.

RAISIN WHIRLS

1 Place the raisins and currants into a bowl and pour the boiling water over them. Leave the fruit to soak for 30 minutes, then strain the hydrated fruit and set to one side.

2 In a small bowl mix together the sugar and spice. Take a half quantity of Danish pastry out of the fridge and unwrap.

3 Flour the work surface and begin to roll out the dough in a lengthwise direction to begin with. You're aiming for a long rectangle approximately 40 x 17cm (15¾ x 6¾in). Keep the top of the dough and rolling pin very lightly floured, and if any butter starts to break through the surface add a scant pinch of flour to it. The dough will naturally widen as the piece lengthens. Keep checking that the dough isn't sticking to the work surface, adding a light dusting of flour if necessary. If the pastry becomes difficult to roll out let it rest for 5 minutes. Try to keep the edges straight, and once you reach the required length adjust the width and it should be just about there. Scatter the spice and sugar mixture over the surface leaving a 2 cm (¾in) section at the bottom clean. Top the sugar with the drained fruits.

4 Start to roll up the pastry from the top of the dough towards you. When you reach the end slightly dampen the clean dough with water and pinch together firmly to seal. Turn the seam so that it sits underneath.

5 Wrap the log in a piece of baking (parchment) paper and chill for 30 minutes in the fridge. Once chilled, unwrap the log and trim off the ends to neaten. Use a serrated bread knife to gently cut the log into 8 whirls, each approximately 2cm (¾in) wide.

6 Place the whirls on lined baking sheets, spaced well apart. Cover and allow to rise for 2 hours until puffy and almost doubled in size. Once risen, place them in the fridge to chill for 30 minutes. Preheat the oven to 190°C (fan)/210°C/425°F/Gas Mark 7.

7 Brush the tops with beaten egg and bake in the oven for 12 minutes until golden. Serve warm.

CROISSANTS

A simple way to use Danish pastry. Half a portion of dough will make 6 croissants. They can also be shaped and frozen ready to defrost and bake for a luxurious breakfast.

MAKES 6 CROISSANTS
PREP ⏲ DANISH PASTRY – 35 MINUTES PLUS 4 HOURS OR OVERNIGHT RESTING | **PREP** ⏲ CROISSANTS – 15 MINUTES PLUS 2½ HOURS PROVING
BAKE ⏲ 15–18 MINUTES | OVEN 190°C (FAN)/210°C/425°F/ GAS MARK 7

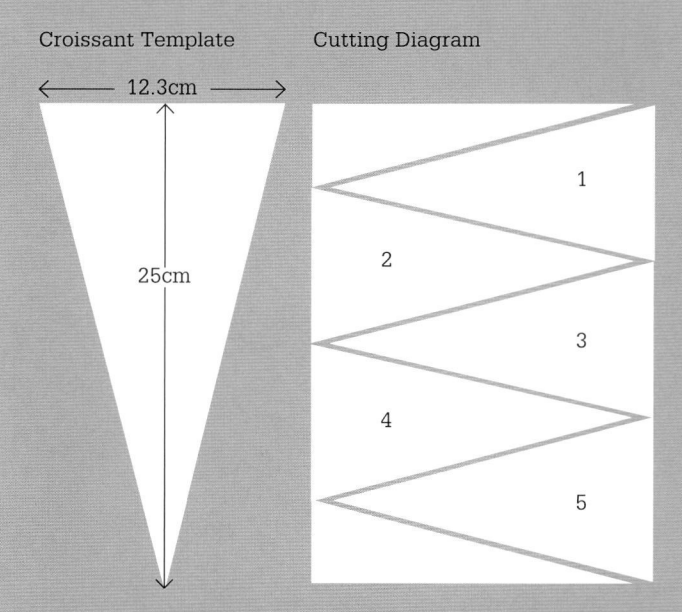

Croissant Template: 12.3cm × 25cm

Cutting Diagram: 5 triangles plus two half-triangles

INGREDIENTS
Half quantity Danish pastry
Flour for dusting
1 egg, beaten

EQUIPMENT
Rolling pin
Ruler
Pizza wheel
Baking sheet

1. Roll out the pastry on a lightly floured work surface to a rectangle measuring 25 x 35cm (10 x 13¾in).

2. Using the diagram as a guide, lightly mark your triangles in the dough surface with a knife.

3. Once you are happy with the position of your triangles, cut the dough using a pizza wheel. You should have 5 triangles plus two half-triangles from the ends. Take the two triangular off cuts at either end and stack them one on top of the other. Roll with the pin to secure them together and gently encourage into a piece big enough to cut out the remaining croissant triangle.

4. Take one triangle at a time and place it with the pointed end facing you. Gently tug the top corners outwards and then roll the triangle up loosely. The thin point should fold over the top and touch the surface but not sit underneath.

5. Transfer the croissants to a well greased baking sheet, cover and allow to rest for 10 minutes. After resting, gently curve the croissants into a crescent shape. Cover again and leave to rise for 2 hours or until nearly doubled in size.

6. Once they are risen, chill them for 30 minutes. Brush them well with beaten egg and bake in the preheated oven for 15–18 minutes until they are a deep golden brown. Serve warm.

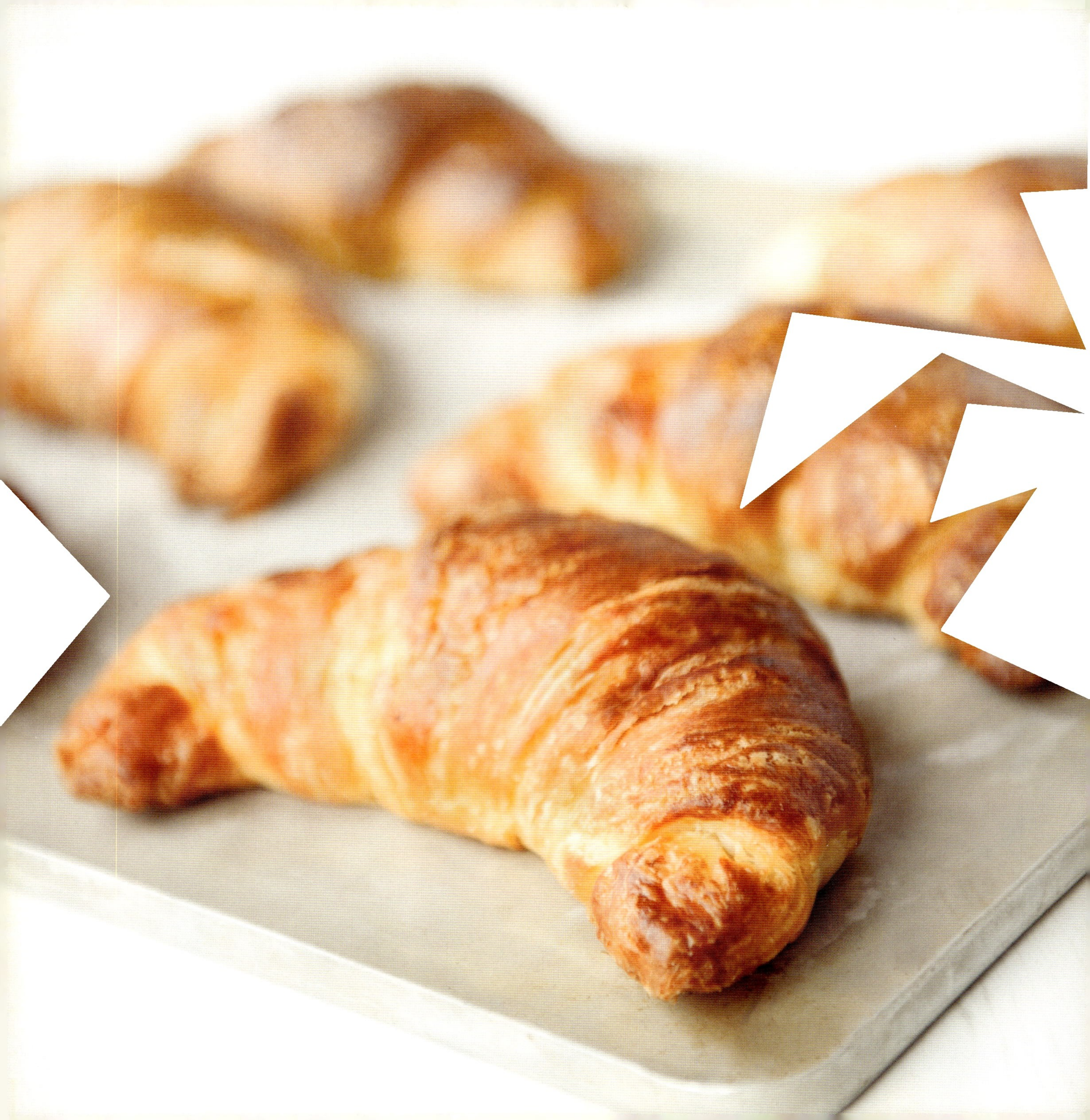

SUPPLIERS

THE PINK WHISK SHOP
www.thepinkwhiskshop.co.uk Tel: 0844 880 5852
For all the baking equipment to get you started – and lots more besides! All products are chosen by me especially for you.

Kenwood Ltd
New Lane,
Havant
Hampshire PO9 2NH
www.kenwoodworld.com/uk
Tel: 02392 476 000
For kitchen electricals.

Wright's Flour
GR Wright & Sons Ltd
Ponders End Mills,
Enfield,
Middlesex EN3 4TG
Tel: 0800 064 0100
www.wrightsflour.co.uk
For British grown and milled flours.

Baking Mad
The Baking Mad Kitchen,
Sugar Way,
Peterborough PE2 9AY
Tel@ 0800 880 5944
www.bakingmad.com
For Silverspoon, Allinson's, Billington's, Nielsen-Massey

Bakery Bits
BakeryBits Ltd
1 Orchard Units
Duchy Road
Honiton
Devon EX14 1YD
Tel: 01404 565656
www.bakerybits.co.uk
For bread baking equipment, dough baskets and other supplies.

NordicWare UK
2 Cherrywood Way
Little Aston
Sutton Coldfield
West Midlands B74 4HZ
Tel/Fax 0121 353 8284
www.nordicware.com
For a great range of bowls, scrapers and metal dough blades.

US
Michaels
Michaels Stores, Inc.
8000 Bent Branch Dr.
Irving TX 75063
Tel: (1-800-642-4235)
www.michaels.com

A C Moore Arts & Crafts
Stores across the US
Tel: 1-888-226-667
www.acmoore.com

Williams-Sonoma
Locations across the US
Tel: 877-812-6235
www.williams-sonoma.com
Bakeware, kitchenware and kitchen electricals.

AUSTRALIA
Kitchen Witch
500 Hay Street
Subiaco WA 6008
Tel: 08 9380 4788
www.homeinwa.com.au

Myer
Stores across Australia
PO Box 869J
Melbourne VIC 3001
Phone: 1800 811 611
For Bakeware and other baking essentials.

Target
Stores across Australia
Customer Relations
Reply Paid 41
Nth Geelong Vic 3215.
Tel: 1800 814 788
www.target.com.au

ABOUT THE AUTHOR

Ruth Clemens is mum of three naughty boys and wife to one! A passionate self-taught baker, bread maker and cake decorator Ruth was a finalist on the very first series of the BBC's *The Great British Bake Off*. Her first book *The Busy Girls' Guide to Cake Decorating* was published in April 2012, followed by *The Pink Whisk Guide to Cake Making* in April 2013.

Ruth writes the popular baking blog The Pink Whisk, which was featured in *The Independent*'s Best Top 50 Food Websites.

To keep up to date with Ruth's most recent adventures you can join the gang and ask any burning queries at facebook.com/ThePinkWhisk or on Twitter @thepinkwhisk – and we'd love to see your bread pics!

For lots more baking inspiration and recipes visit **www.thepinkwhisk.co.uk**

ACKNOWLEDGEMENTS

So many people to thank – all of whom have been force-fed sandwiches in the search for the perfect bread recipes.

To Damian, Ashley, Dylan and Finlay, my toast-eating gang of boys.

David & Charles and the FW Media team for their support: Verity, Pru, Ame, Ali and Katy.

Lorna and Jack for the gorgeous photos, making every loaf come alive on the page, just the way I imagined it.

To Kenwood for the loan of a Pink Boutique K-Mix – no Pink Whisking, but the dough hook has been invaluable and rescued my tired arms many a time!

My huge thanks to Wright's for a supply of fantastic flour that has made every recipe work just the way it should – Wright's produce British grown and milled flours and their strong white, wholemeal and malted flours are my flours of choice.

To Silver Spoon, Billington's and Allinson's for the extra ingredients that transform many of the recipes into something special and made many of these loaves possible.

A great big thank you to Louise Brimelow for her invaluable help on the photo shoot.

And lastly, the biggest thank you of all is to the troops known as 'The Pink Whiskers' – readers of the blog, with their boundless amounts of encouragement and support. We may only have met digitally but you're all welcome round my way for bread and butter pudding any day of the week! xx

Suppliers 125

INDEX

apple Danish plait 76–9

bacon & cheese potato bread 48–51
bagels 96–101
   sweet cinnamon & cranberry 102–3
baking technique 16–17
basic loaves
   brown 28–9
   white 20–7
BBQ twist & swirl loaf 36–9
braided herby loaf 110–11
brioche 112–15
   pizza 116–17
brown loaf, basic 28–9

cake tins 9
'cakey' bread 19
challah 104–9
cheese & bacon potato bread 48–51
chilli & chorizo potato bread 52–3
chocolate
   & hazelnut wheel 92–3
   orange spiced fingers 54–7
chorizo & chilli potato bread 52–3
ciabatta with olive oil 82–5
cinnamon
   & cranberry bagels 102–3
   twist & swirl loaf 40–1
cobb, crusty 62–7
cooling bread 17
cranberry
   & cinnamon bagels 102–3
   & Stilton wheel 88–91
croissants 122–3
crusty bread, how to get 17

crusty cobb 62–7

Danish apple plait 76–9
Danish pastry
   croissants 122–3
   raisin whirls 118–21
dough
   rough 12
   shaping 14–15
   spine 14–15

egg 'n' ham filling, picnic plait 80–1
equipment 8–9

fats 11
fingers
   iced lemon 58–9
   spiced chocolate orange 54–7
flours 10
foccacia, rosemary & sea salt 86–7
freezing bread 17
fruit breads
   raisin whirls 118–21
   teacakes 34–5

glazing bread 16

ham 'n' egg filling, picnic plait 80–1
hazelnut & chocolate wheel 92–3
herby braided loaf 110–11
honey oat rolls 46–7

iced lemon fingers 58–9
ingredients 10–11

kneading 12–13
knocking back 14

lemon iced fingers 58–9
liquids 11
loaves
   bacon & cheese potato 48–51
   basic brown 28–9
   basic white 20–7
   BBQ twist & swirl 36–9
   brioche 112–15
   challah 104–9
   chorizo & chilli potato 52–3
   ciabatta with olive oil 82–5
   cinnamon twist & swirl 40–1
   crusty cobb 62–7
   herby braided 110–11
   malthouse 42–5
   maple & pecan 74–5
   picnic plait 80–1
   rosemary & sea salt foccacia 86–7
   seeded multigrain 70–3
   Stilton & cranberry wheel 88–91
   tiger bread 68–9
malthouse loaf 42–5
maple & pecan loaf 74–5
multigrain seeded loaf 70–3

oat honey rolls 46–7
orange chocolate spiced fingers 54–7

pecan & maple loaf 74–5
picnic plait 80–1
pizza, brioche 116–17
plaits
   challah 104–9
   Danish apple 76–9
   herby braided loaf 110–11
   picnic 80–1
potato bread
   bacon & cheese 48–51
   chorizo & chilli 52–3
pre-ferment 12, 60–93
proving baskets 15
proving/rising
   first 13–14
   second 15–16

raisin whirls 118–21
refreshing bread 17
rolls 15
   honey oat 46–7
   quick white 30–3
rosemary & sea salt foccacia 86–7

salt 11
seeded multigrain loaf 70–3
slashing bread 16
spiced chocolate orange fingers 54–7
spine (dough) 14–15
Stilton & cranberry wheel 88–91
storing bread 17
sugar 11
sweet breads
   chocolate & hazelnut wheel 92–3
   cinnamon twist & swirl loaf 40–1
   Danish apple plait 76–9
   iced lemon fingers 58–9
   maple & pecan loaf 74–5
   raisin whirls 118–21
   spiced chocolate orange fingers 54–7
   sweet cinnamon & cranberry bagels 102–3
   teacakes 34–5

teacakes 34–5
thermometer probes 17
tiger bread 68–9
troubleshooting 18–19
twist & swirl loaves
   BBQ 36–9
   cinnamon 40–1

wheels
   chocolate & hazelnut 92–3
   Stilton & cranberry 88–91
whirls, raisin 118–21
white basic loaf 20–7
white quick rolls 30–3

yeast 10–11

Metric and imperial measurements are given for the recipes in this book. Use one set of measurements only, not a mixture of both.

Level spoon measurements have been used throughout, where 1tsp = 5ml and 1tbsp = 15ml.

Ovens should be pre-heated to the required temperature before use.

Some recipes contain nuts or nut derivatives. These recipes should not be eaten by those with known nut allergies, or by those who may be vulnerable to such allergies.

A DAVID & CHARLES BOOK
© F&W Media International, LTD 2013

David & Charles is an imprint of F&W Media International, LTD
Brunel House, Forde Close, Newton Abbot, TQ12 4PU, UK

F&W Media International, Ltd is a subsidiary of F+W Media, Inc
10151 Carver Road, Suite #200, Blue Ash, OH 45242, USA

Text and designs copyright © Ruth Clemens 2013
Photography and illustrations © F&W Media International, LTD 2013

First published in the UK & USA in 2013
Digital edition published in 2013

Ruth Clemens has asserted her right to be identified as author of this work in accordance with the Copyright, Designs and Patents Act, 1988.

All rights reserved. No part of this publication may be reproduced in any form or by any means, electronic or mechanical, by photocopying, recording or otherwise, without prior permission in writing from the publisher.

The author and publisher have made every effort to ensure that all the instructions in the book are accurate and safe, and therefore cannot accept liability for any resulting injury, damage or loss to persons or property, however it may arise.

Names of manufacturers, products and product ranges are provided for the information of readers, with no intention to infringe copyright or trademarks.

A catalogue record for this book is available from the British Library.

ISBN-13: 978-1-4463-0280-4 Hardback
ISBN-10: 1-4463-0280-6 Hardback

ISBN-13: 978-1-4463-0326-9 Paperback
ISBN-10: 1-4463-0326-8 Paperback

10 9 8 7 6 5 4 3 2 1

Publisher Alison Myer
Junior Acquisitions Editor Verity Graves-Morris
Project Editor Katy Denny
Creative Manager Prudence Rogers
Production Manager Bev Richardson
Photographer Lorna Yabsley / Jack Kirby

Printed in China by RR Donnelley for:
F&W Media International LTD,
Brunel House, Forde Close, Newton Abbot, TQ12 4PU, UK

F+W Media publishes high quality books on a wide range of subjects.
For more great book ideas visit: www.stitchcraftcreate.co.uk